DESIGN ON FABRICS

DESIGN
ON FABRICS

Meda Parker Johnston

Glen Kaufman

VAN NOSTRAND REINHOLD COMPANY

New York   Cincinnati   Toronto   London   Melbourne

Van Nostrand Reinhold Company Regional Offices:
New York Cincinnati Chicago Millbrae Dallas

Van Nostrand Reinhold Company International Offices:
London Toronto Melbourne

Copyright © 1967 by LITTON EDUCATIONAL
PUBLISHING, INC.
Library of Congress Catalog Card Number 66-22689
ISBN 0-442-24170-4

Designed by Emilio Squeglio

Published by Van Nostrand Reinhold Company
450 West 33rd Street, New York, N.Y. 10001

Published simultaneously in Canada by
Van Nostrand Reinhold Ltd.

16 15 14 13 12 11 10 9 8 7

Contents

Introduction

The subject of this book is the embellishment of fabric surface by means of dye or pigment: in a phrase, fabric decoration. Throughout its long history fabric decoration has made a significant contribution to the cultural heritage of countless civilizations, and it continues to be a dynamic force today.

The story of fabric decoration is a story of design. The two cannot be separated, but must be considered as one. We have not attempted to provide an outline in basic design, since excellent material on this subject is available in other volumes. Rather, an attempt has been made to relate generally agreed upon design basics to fabric decoration, with the hope that each craftsman working with the techniques covered in this book will develop his personal approach and achieve personal solutions.

Special emphasis is given to the materials and processes of fabric decoration with the desire that the craftsman understand their unique potentials, learn to control them, and use them to express his individuality.

Both the inexperienced and the practiced craftsman have been considered in the planning of this book. It is meant to be a guide in a way that suits each person.

It should be noted that a Glossary of technical terms has been provided.

A book of this nature is not possible without the help of many individuals, each contributing in a special way. We wish to thank the students who have asked many questions and provided many answers over the several years during which the book has developed. Many examples of their work illustrate the volume. Our appreciation goes to the individual craftsmen and manufacturers who have supplied information and photographs. It also goes to the outstanding museums that have been most cooperative in providing photographs of work in their collections. Special thanks are due to Alice Baldwin Beer of The Cooper Union Museum for her encouragement and complete cooperation, and to George Fuller for the line drawings that are included in the book. Finally, we are indeed grateful for the many valuable contributions our editor, Nancy C. Newman, has made.

1. History of Fabric Decoration

Origins of Fabric Decoration

From the earliest recorded history, man has decorated the fabric surfaces of his environment. Perhaps his clothing was decorated first, then other items necessary to his existence. Although it may be impossible to pinpoint the beginning of this art, it is obvious from the available evidence that it was an important development in cultures widely separated in time and geographic location.

Numerous attempts to explain the origins of fabric decoration have resulted in a variety of theories. It has been proposed that early cultures of hunters and planters evolved characteristic designs which were used in the hope of favorably influencing their lives, e.g. improving the hunt or crops. Decoration may also have served as a means of identification within and between cultural groups. Other designs may have occurred by accident, such as a hand- or footprint of mud or clay on fabric, and it is possible that natural materials such as leaves, twigs, or stones were used to apply a colorant to cloth.*

Whatever the origin of the earliest fabrics decorated with colorant, it is obvious that fabric decoration has been a significant and dynamic force in man's cultural history. Religion, economics, and psychology have been or are factors in the continued development of this aspect of the fabric arts.

While no decorated fabrics exist from the earliest known cultures, other artifacts indicate the existence of embellished surfaces. Archaeological investigations have brought to light a variety of stamps that may have been used for printing fabric in Mesopotamia 5,000 years ago. Some of the stamps that have been found are cylinder and rocker shapes, and others are flat with a handle on the back, indicating a variety of uses.

Other evidence of decorated fabric has been found in early civilizations of this culturally rich area. Babylonians and Assyrians used patterns in sculptured representations of clothing textiles. From cultures in this area the arts of fabric decoration spread and were adapted to their new environments, producing a variety of distinct styles.

Further indirect evidence of decorated fabrics is found in Egyptian mural paintings dating from as early as 2500 B.C. The motifs are geometric in design and are used in repeat, possibly the result of a stamping technique. No fabrics thus decorated have survived. Specimens of hieroglyphs painted on fabric dating from 1545-1350 B.C. have been found, as well as resist-painted and mordant-dyed mummy cloths from before 1000 B.C. This early activity was followed by block printing, described in historical accounts as early as the fifth century B.C., and the use of clay or wax resists combined with refined mordant dyeing. It is believed that some of these dyeing techniques traveled to Egypt along trade routes from India.

Pliny the Elder (23-79 A.D.), a Roman writer, described a complicated dyeing process in a section of his *Natural History* entitled "A Remarkable Process":

Moreover in Egypt they have a device to stain cloths . . . which they besmear not with colours but with certain drugs that are apt to drink and take colour: when they have so done, there is no appearance in them at all of any dye or tincture. These clothes they cast into a lead or cauldron of some colour that is seething and scalding hot: where, after they have remained a pretty while, they take them forth again, all stained and painted in sundry colours. An admirable thing, that there being in the said cauldron but only one kind of tincture, yet out of it the cloth should be

*W. Born, "Textile Ornament," *Ciba Review* #37, January, 1941, pp. 1322-26.

stained with this and that colour, and the foresaid boiling liquor change so as it doth, according to the quality and nature of the drugs which were laid upon the white first. And verily, these stains or colours are set so sure, as they can never be washed off afterwards.*

Asia

India, perhaps, has had the longest continuous history of decorating fabrics with dyes. Printing blocks dating from 3000 B.C. have been found; they form the foundation on which the rich fabric culture of the country has been built. Indian printed cottons and silks have been marketed throughout the world and have had great influence on both the economy and the aesthetics of many countries. No other country has had so strong an impact on the history of dye-decorated fabrics.

Records dating from 400 B.C. indicate that colored chintzes were common. The word "chintz" is derived from the Hindu *chint*, meaning colored or variegated. The Greek physician Ctesias, writing of India about 400 B.C., alluded to resist-dyed and hand-painted fabrics. Early colors may have been made with fruit, flower, root, or bark stains that were made fast by the addition of acid soil or mud containing iron. Out of these early procedures grew the now complicated chemistry of dyeing.

In 327 B.C., when India was invaded by Alexander the Great, colorful printed cottons were again described by the Greeks. As a result of such invasions and the establishment of trade routes, printed and painted Indian cottons became known in the wider world of Asia and beyond. In the second century A.D. Arab traders brought Indian printed cottons to Europe via the Red Sea. Two centuries later, Indian merchants and sailors who settled in Java introduced wax resist techniques which developed into the highly individualistic "batiks" of that area.

A significant number of Indian fabrics has been recovered, many of them from the ruins of Fostat (Old Cairo), Egypt. They date, roughly, from the twelfth to fifteenth centuries A.D. and give evidence of the lively trade between the two countries. Many of these fabrics were block printed with resist and dyed either with blue (indigo) or red (madder). The designs are striking in their directness and simplicity—qualities that grew out of the technique used. They are, for the most part, two-color prints consisting of the natural color of the cotton ground and either blue or red, some with tints of these colors resulting from several dyeings. As a result of the resist approach, the backgrounds were dyed

Resist block print on cotton, India, 14th-15th century. Found in Fostat, Egypt. (Courtesy of The Cooper Union Museum)

Resist block print on wood, India, 15th century. (The Metropolitan Museum of Art, Gift of V. Everit Macy, 1929)

darker in color than the motif, which remained the lighter color of the ground cloth.

When Vasco da Gama discovered a sea route to India in the sixteenth century, Indian textiles had assumed a more intricate and exotic quality which quickly attracted the interest of the Europeans. For a number of years Portuguese and Spanish traders had a virtual monopoly of the distribution of Indian calicoes both to other Asian countries and to Europe. Calicoes were named after the seaport of Calicut in southwest Madras from which many were exported. In the late sixteenth century, with the establishment of the British East India Company, other European traders imported the Indian cottons to a growing market in the West. This brought about great changes in the production of printed fabric in Europe.

The designs of the calicoes contrasted sharply with the earlier resist prints. The fabrics were brilliant in a wide variety of fresh colors, and the motifs

* Philemon Holland (trans.), *The Natural History of C. Plinius Secundus* (Carbondale, Illinois, 1962), p. 427.

employed were complex, often without definite repeat. Flowers, plants, trees, and vines in fine detail were combined with animal and sometimes human figures, with exotic polychrome effects. The individual pieces frequently contained a large central motif (e.g. a fantastic tree growing from rocks or earth inhabited by peacocks and other fauna) surrounded by a border of flowers, small trees, or trailing vines. These fabrics were used as bedcovers, valances, or wall hangings rather than for clothing.

The techniques employed were as complicated as the designs and required a comprehensive knowledge of dye chemistry to achieve brilliant and lasting results. A Jesuit priest, Father Coeurdoux, described a method of decorating cottons in letters dated 1742. Following is a brief summary of his account. First, the cloth was prepared by a bleaching and mordanting process using an extract of a dry fruit called cadou and buffalo milk. The design was then applied to the fabric by pouncing charcoal dust through a perforated paper cartoon. Next, the design was outlined with a brush using black iron and red dye. Indigo was used for blue, and all areas not to be affected had to be covered with wax before dipping in the blue dyebath. Then the wax was removed, the cloth washed and mordanted again, and other colors applied. The process was repeated for each color that was added, with areas waxed to preserve colors already applied. Father Coeurdoux gave detailed accounts of each operation and descriptions of the specific plant or mineral materials used for each color.*

The eyewitness account gives a clear idea of the mastery these craftsmen had over the intricate dyeing process—a mastery that was long envied in Europe and that was approached there only after decades of experimentation. It was the Indian painted calico that set the standards of design and technical achievement for many years after its arrival in the West.

Some years after the Indian printed cottons first found a receptive market in Europe, strong influences were felt that had detrimental effects upon their design. As a result of the great demand for calicoes, methods had to be altered to shorten the production time. Much of the hand painting was replaced by block printing, and designs were simplified by utilizing repeated motifs. Europeans placed special orders requesting the inclusion of family crests and armorial bearings commemorating spe-

Coverlet or hanging, painted and dyed, India, 18th century. (Courtesy of The Cooper Union Museum)

Painted and dyed cotton, India, 17th century. (Courtesy of The Cooper Union Museum)

* MacIver Percival, *The Chintz Book* (New York, n.d.), pp. 10-12.

Sari, tie-dyed cotton, India, ca. 19th century. (Courtesy of The Brooklyn Museum)

Tie-dyed silk, Japan, 16th-17th century.

cial events, and the designs on the fabrics began to change from their original indigenous character to incorporate extraneous elements and motifs.

In addition to the painted and printed fabrics that became known in many areas of the world, there were other traditional Indian techniques that were employed in the embellishment of cloth surfaces. One that was highly developed but found little interest among Europeans was tie-dye, or *bhandana*, in which sections of the fabric were bound tightly before dyeing, creating a design through resist. The effects achieved with this approach were generally abstract, unlike those of drawing or painting with which Westerners were familiar. The technique was also difficult to imitate. The one exception may have been the bandanna handkerchief, ornamented with white spots on a blue or red ground, which was developed by the Europeans.

Early in its history, China developed sophisticated cultures in which fabric decoration was a significant art. Block printing is thought to have originated as early as 400 B.C., and further developments in fabric printing took place during the Han Period (206 B.C.-220 A.D.). The techniques of silk weaving and embroidery were also highly developed in China, and they overshadowed approaches that utilized dyes and pigments for embellishment. The latter techniques, however, as well as weaving, were introduced to Japan beginning in the third or fourth century A.D. and became highly developed national arts in their new environment.

Few fabrics exist from the primitive age of Japanese cultural history, although there is some indica-

tion of simple geometric ornamentation on clothing from the evidence of terra-cotta tomb figures. Not until the eighth century A.D. did Japan produce a variety of decorated fabrics, and much of it was a result of Chinese influence, which reached a high point in the T'ang Period (618-907 A.D.). Frequently the importation of fabric prototypes from China resulted in frustration, because the technology needed to adapt them to Japanese use was lacking.

During the Nara Period (710-784 A.D.) in Japan, however, fabric was decorated with stamped, painted, and stenciled patterns, and the technique of wax resist was used. A unique method called jam-dyeing was also employed. The cloth was folded in two and jammed between two wooden boards that were perforated in a design, and dye was poured on the perforations.

The decorated fabric was used primarily for clothing (this has been the case up to recent times), and the designs consisted of symmetrical patterns or regular repeats of the same motif, with polychrome effects.

About the twelfth century the kimono began to develop as the national dress of Japan, and new types of decoration, characterized by large-scale, free motifs, were used to embellish it.

Between the fourteenth and sixteenth centuries foreign influences again had a great impact on Japanese fabric decoration. The importation of fabrics from China during the Ming Period (1348-1644) led to more experiments with graphic designs that could readily be realized with dye work. Motifs utilizing flowering plants, flowers and birds, and animals were developed and refined in painting and stencil work. These pictures drawn on fabric used for clothing showed no feeling for the relationship between patterned surface and the function of the fabric.

Another strong influence on Japan in the mid-sixteenth century was that of the Indian calicoes introduced by Portuguese and Dutch traders. The Indian printed cottons were popular with the upper classes primarily for their use as linings or undergarments; the poorer classes used them to cover small boxes and other items. The calicoes revealed an entirely different approach to Japanese craftsmen. The designs were suggestive rather than literal, abstract rather than realistic. The scale of the designs was frequently much smaller than that employed to decorate the kimono.

Two types of fabric were produced in Japan as a result of the importation of Indian cottons: hand-blocked prints in indigenous colors and designs, and hand-painted copies which were of poor quality because Japanese dye technology was inadequate.

In the Edo Period (1673-1801) Japanese craftsmen developed numerous decoration techniques. Among these was starch-resist dyeing, which was used to decorate the kimono in free designs. Since the style of the kimono was established by custom, one was distinguished from another by its embellishment. This led to an endless variety of designs, and seldom if ever were any two exactly alike.

A part of Japan that produced distinctive techniques and designs is Ryukyu, a group of fifty islands (including Okinawa) 400 miles south of the main Japanese islands. Although somewhat isolated from the mainstream of Japanese culture, Ryukyu had periodic contact with China, Korea, and parts of Southeast Asia.

Stencil dyeing was highly developed and used in combination with resists and hand painting. Natural dyes known elsewhere were native to the islands: indigo, cochineal, and other plant and mineral ex-

Stencils for printing textiles, paper, Japan, 1615-1867. (The Metropolitan Museum of Art, Gift of Clarence McK. Lewis, 1953)

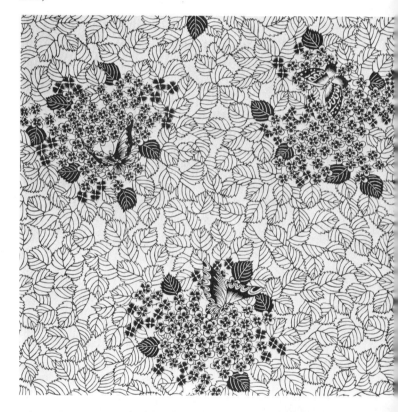

Sarong, batik on cotton, Java, 19th century. (The Metropolitan Museum of Art, Gift of Mrs. John Stemme, 1919)

tracts produced a wide range of colors. Techniques and designs were used and refined over many centuries in Ryukyu, but they were considered primitive compared to methods used in Japan proper.

As noted earlier, Indian traders introduced resist dyeing techniques to Java about 400 A.D. These were developed over many centuries into a unique decorative technique commonly known as batik. In batik hot wax is applied to a fabric which is then dyed; the wax is removed, and the design revealed. A characteristic line or edge results from this technique, and in some pieces a unique crackle effect is realized by controlled manipulation of the waxed cloth before or during dyeing.

Four general types of resist techniques were developed in Indonesia: the application of rice-starch paste with the fingers, sticks, or leaves; bamboo stick batik, in which wax and resin are spread on cloth with a stick; the use of the tjanting, a special tool consisting of a handle and a reservoir with a spout or spouts, to apply hot wax; and the use of the tjap, a metal stamp, which is dipped in hot wax and printed on cloth.

The dyes used were limited in color range, the most common being indigo, which produced variations of blue, and rich browns. Other colors were used later, but the outstanding fabrics were created in a few colors with subtle variations.

The decorated fabrics were used primarily for sarongs, the native dress, and the designs employed a variety of indigenous motifs. Geometric motifs were dominant and were combined with representations of plant or animal life. The batiks were produced in limited numbers; cheap imitations were not made, and an active export market did not develop.

Other techniques were also developed in Indonesia, some of them combined with batik. Painting and tie-dye (*plangi*) were common, as well as another resist technique called *tri-tik*, in which the design was stitched on the fabric. The stitches resisted the dye, creating the design.

Sarong, batik on cotton, Java, 19th-20th century. (The Metropolitan Museum of Art, Bequest of Helen W. D. Mileham, 1954)

Child's dress, painted tapa, Celebes Islands, 20th century. (Cranbrook Institute of Science)

Europe

Fabrics from Asia and Africa were known in medieval Europe through travel and trade, but perhaps because dye technology was lacking, there was little attempt to duplicate the luxurious imported cloths. It was not until the eleventh century that there appears to have been any concentrated activity in fabric printing. Wood-block printing was developed in Germany for book illustration and as a cheap means of reproducing the designs of woven brocades, damasks, and velvets that were both admired and expensive. At first the blocks were small, but in time larger blocks were developed, and they increased production capabilities. The effort to imitate a woven fabric or subtle hand-painted cotton runs through the history of fabric decoration in the West for many centuries.

Since knowledge of dyes was limited in Europe, the early printers relied on pigments to embellish fabric surfaces. Black was frequently printed on natural linen ground as well as on colored fabric. Gum or some other sticky substance was printed to adhere gilding or silvering to fabric, creating some feeling of luxury.

Since the materials available were limited, the printers sought variety in motif to enhance their patterned cloths. The designs of German fabrics of the twelfth century show Byzantine and Near Eastern influences on subject matter and pattern. Pairs of animals were used, frequently with foliage, producing a free-flowing pattern. Other designs employed the same subject matter enclosed within pointed oval frames which were repeated, giving an allover effect. Stylized leaves, flowers, and fruits, as well as geometric motifs, were also copied from woven fabrics.

The art of fabric printing continued to develop and be refined through the sixteenth century. Designs became more complex and more detailed in pattern. As economic conditions improved, the demand for cheap printed imitations diminished, although it never disappeared. It was a propitious time for the introduction of a new stimulus to fabric printing.

As a result of the opening of trade routes to India, first by Portugal and then by other European countries, calicoes became available in Europe and were enthusiastically received. These cloths were called "pintadoes" and "indiennes" in Portugal and France respectively.

In 1631 the East India Company was granted permission to import the cottons to England, and they were an immediate success. There had previously been block printing on fabric in England, probably related to similar activity on the continent, especially in Germany. In 1676 William Sherwin was granted permission to print cottons by the Indian method using wooden blocks. Of course, knowledge of dye chemistry was limited, and the result was poor imitations of the originals. A method for printing flocking on silk, leather, and cotton as a cheap substitute for velvet, developed some years earlier, had had the same result. However, the wool and silk merchants were unhappy with the competition, and in 1700 the importation of Indian printed goods was prohibited. Despite the ban, the use of Indian calicoes and English copies increased and in some cases led to riots in which weavers and their supporters attacked women who wore printed cottons.

Block print, silver pigment on linen, Germany, 12th-14th century. (Courtesy of The Cooper Union Museum)

Block print, black pigment on linen, Germany, 13th century. (Courtesy of The Cooper Union Museum)

Resist block print on linen, Germany, 17th century. (Courtesy of The Cooper Union Museum)

Printed cotton, England, ca. 1820-30. (Courtesy of The Art Institute of Chicago)

Copperplate print on linen and cotton, England, ca. 1790. (The Metropolitan Museum of Art, Bequest of Charles Allen Munn, 1924)

Printed cotton, England, dated 1761. (Courtesy of The Art Institute of Chicago)

The business of printing flourished in England in the early eighteenth century as dye techniques and their application were mastered. Further efforts were made to prohibit the manufacture of calicoes, but freedom to print on pure cotton was granted in 1774. With this recognition of printing as a true industry came further development. In the 1770's the roller was introduced in fabric printing and greatly increased the output of the industry. It did limit the length of the repeat and the scale of design, however, and because of these limitations, block printing continued to be used for furnishings fabrics.

Another innovation in the printing industry that had a great impact on the design and production of fabrics was the copperplate, developed by Francis Nixon in Ireland about 1750. The designs were usually printed in one color (red or blue) on a natural ground. The motifs were complete "pictures" repeated in simple and obvious ways. The subject matter consisted largely of pastoral or classical landscapes, groups of figures or *chinoiseries* (what the English presumed to be Chinese). The designs reflected not only the fashions but also the events of the time—adventure on the seas, the excavation of classical cities, and military campaigns. It is not difficult to understand these sources of design as we witness similar reflections of interests and events in our fabrics in the twentieth century.

The printed fabrics with large-scale designs were widely used in home furnishings, while smaller patterns were employed for clothing fabrics. As the market increased, so did technical developments in the chemistry of dyes and the production of cloth. Industrialization of fabric printing continued in the nineteenth century and led to the revolt by William Morris in the 1870's.

Morris, student of architecture, poet, writer, craftsman, and avid socialist, was cofounder, with John Ruskin, of the Arts and Crafts movement. He worked in a number of crafts, among them fabric printing, and he stressed knowledge of the materials and the process as a means of humanizing the life of his time. His designs were largely based on nature. He wrote, "I must have unmistakable suggestions of gardens and fields, strange trees, boughs and tendrils. . . ."* Contemporary with Morris' last designs for printed fabrics were those of the Art Nouveau movement, which also had significant influence on the art of fabric decoration.

The introduction of Indian calicoes to France in the seventeenth century and the subsequent history of the fabrics follow very closely the developments in England already described. They became popular very quickly, were opposed by the weaving industry and prohibited, but managed to increase in popularity, production, and sales. The early copies of the Indian prints in France were accomplished with the

"Daffodils and Crocus," by Arthur Wilcock, roller print England, ca. 1890. (Courtesy of The Cooper Union Museum)

"Windrush," by William Morris, block print on cotton, England, 1883. (Courtesy of The Cooper Union Museum)

* Graeme Shankland, "William Morris Designer," in Asa Briggs (ed.), *William Morris Selected Writings and Designs* (Baltimore, 1962).

Block print, *Toile de Jouy*, France, ca. 1775. (Courtesy of The Cooper Union Museum)

use of pigments because the knowledge of dye chemistry was very limited. These cloths were not outstanding in design or in technical accomplishment.

The name of Oberkampf and the *Toiles de Jouy* he developed stand at the apex of French fabric printing art. Christophe-Philippe Oberkampf was born in Germany in 1738 to a family long involved in the dyeing and printing crafts. His father had worked for many years to develop a successful resist print method and in the 1740's achieved his goal.

Young Oberkampf traveled to France and worked in chintz printing. In 1759 he set up the historic print works at Jouy, a short distance from Paris. Oberkampf was responsible for the complete operation, from design to finishing of the cloth. The largest part of his production was single-color copperplate prints, the earliest in red dyes. By the end of the eighteenth century the business was thriving, and he was producing complicated designs in a number of colors, using both blocks and copperplates. Oberkampf traveled about Europe evaluating his markets, seeking new designs, and buying cloth. He received French royal sanction and patronage, which added greatly to his prestige and prosperity. Early in the nineteenth century rollers were employed for printing at Jouy, greatly increasing the capacity of the print works.

Oberkampf's success depended to a great extent on his ability to provide designs that were readily acceptable and on his use of inventions and innovations that had been developed elsewhere. He was sensitive to the particular tastes of the moment and was able to satisfy them on short notice. He frequently used *chinoiserie* designs. Later, peasant scenes and other pastoral themes dominated his work, followed by allegorical designs or designs based on mythology. Political events did not escape his attention: both the French and American revolutions provided subject matter for printed cloth. It was possible to change elements in a stock pattern to play upon last-minute developments in historical and political matters.

The effect of printing "pictures" was to create a delicate texture rather than a pattern on the fabrics, especially when they were draped. It was an approach to design that paid little heed to the final use of the cloth, and by present standards may be judged ineffective design.

There was other activity in the decoration of fabric in France. Abstract or floral motifs were repeated to create an effective pattern on fabric to be used in a variety of ways. Some of the more striking examples of this work were done with resist techniques in strong indigo blue, creating simple, direct, and positive designs. It was Oberkampf, however, who made the lasting impression, and whose original *Toile de Jouy* designs are available and furnish interiors today.

Resist print on linen, France, 19th century. (The Metropolitan Museum of Art, Rogers Fund, 1924)

Wood-block print on cotton, *chinoiserie*, France, 18th century. (The Metropolitan Museum of Art, Rogers Fund, 1924)

"La Chasse," by Horace Vernet, *Toile de Jouy*, copperplate print on cotton, France, 1815. (The Metropolitan Museum of Art, Rogers Fund, 1913)

Resist print on cotton, France, 18th century. (Courtesy of The Art Institute of Chicago)

19

Block prints on linen, *noboyka*, Russia, 16th-18th century.
(Courtesy of The Brooklyn Museum)

Between the sixteenth and eighteenth centuries a significant group of prints known as *noboyka* (printed calico) were evolved in Great Russia. These fabrics were printed from wood blocks with vegetable colors on rough linen. Other fabrics of this period, upon examination, appear to have been printed with pigments. They were used for clothes, vestments, standards, tents, curtains, tablecloths, and bookbindings. The first printers were probably painters of icons who were familiar with the decoration of flat surfaces. Later, special groups of craftsmen traveled from village to village printing fabrics to suit the needs of the market.*

The unique quality of these prints is a directness and simplicity that grow out of an honest utilization of the wood-block technique. The prints show an understanding of the potentials and limitations of the technique. Much of the design quality is a result of the mark of the tool cutting the wood surface, which gives a fresh and spontaneous look to the work. The motifs are frequently based on floral, geometric, or pictorial themes, with a repeated design creating a flowing pattern.

L'Art Rustique en Russie (Paris, 1912), p. 10.

Resist stencil print and cassava paste on cotton, Nigeria, 20th century. (Courtesy of The Cooper Union Museum)

Tie-dye, indigo on cotton, Nigeria, 20th century. (Courtesy of The Cooper Union Museum)

Africa

A number of fabric decorating techniques have long been used in the cultures of central Africa. The first decorated fabrics were probably painted directly with the fingers or a simple brush. The motifs fall into three general categories (more than one may be combined in a single fabric). There are those that tell a story, those that have symbolic significance or that serve as identification, and those that are simple ornamentation with a pattern.

Fabric printed with a plant-leaf stencil or stamps made of stick or sections of calabash is also found. The fabric printed with calabash, made by the Ashanti of Ghana and known as *Adinkra cloth*, generally consists of a variety of stamped designs repeated in a rectangular grid. Some of the motifs fit together in an allover repeat, while others are more isolated.

Tie-dye is also used, especially in Nigeria, to create strong, simple designs of a geometric nature. Printing with resist pastes has a long tradition and is done effectively with indigo, occasionally incorporating crackle effects.

Block print, tar on dyed cotton, *Adinkra cloth*, Ghana, Ashanti, 20th century. (Courtesy of The Cooper Union Museum)

21

The Americas

In the Americas the cultures which play the largest part in the history of the fabric arts are those of pre-Columbian Peru. The craftsmen of these early civilizations made outstanding contributions both in fabric structure and ornamentation (needlework and color application). Various Peruvian civilizations separated by time and geography practiced fabric decoration with dyes and pigments in techniques which were similar, yet developed independently. Among these painting and tie-dye were primary.

Although there is no proof as yet, it has been suggested that some of the repeat motifs used to decorate fabrics between 700 and 1100 A.D. may have been executed with hand stamps, rollers, or primitive stencils which have been found. However, few if any fabrics exist which indicate beyond doubt that such devices were used.

Many of the examples of painted fabric that exist today indicate that the craftsmen had a feeling for and an understanding of motif repetition to create an effective surface pattern. The motifs are frequently enclosed in rectangles and make use of negative and positive areas to create the over-all design. The designs include abstract and stylized animals, birds, and human figures, as well as geometric shapes. They are frequently done in prints of one color on fine cotton, while other examples utilize a variety of colors, giving a more complex effect.

Tie-dye was used as a decorating technique on closely woven fabrics and open gauze weaves. Some designs were carefully controlled repeats, while others were more random and free in approach. One method which was unique to Peru incorporated tie-dyed stepped triangles arranged in a patchwork, creating a repeat design of intriguing complexity.

Later South and Central American cultures used stamps and rollers for decorating fabrics. Indigenous groups in the Americas, from South America to the northwest coast of Canada, employed techniques of hand painting on a variety of fabric materials or substitutes such as leather and hide, though none reached the excellence of the Peruvians. After the Spanish conquest, many Peruvian techniques were used to produce fabric designs dictated by the Spanish.

Painted cotton, Peru, 1100-1400. (The Textile Museum, Washington, D.C.)

Painted cotton, Peru, 1100-1400. (The Textile Museum, Washington, D.C.)

22

Tie-dyed alpaca(?), Peru, Tiahuanaco Period, ca. 700-1100. (The Textile Museum, Washington, D.C.)

Painted shirt, Peru, Chimu Culture, ca. 1100-1500. (Courtesy of The Brooklyn Museum)

Wood-block print on cotton, United States(?), 18th century. (The Metropolitan Museum of Art, Gift of Norman M. Isham, 1933)

Printed cotton, United States, 19th century. (Courtesy of The Art Institute of Chicago)

In 1770 calico was first printed in the United States by John Heuson of Philadelphia. The process and designs were direct imports from Europe, for immigrants brought their trades and skills to America. The American industry grew gradually, and by 1811 there were printers established in Philadelphia and New Jersey, which became printing centers, and in other locations. However, many printed fabrics were imported from England and France to meet the demands of the American market. Special commemorative designs were rushed to American merchants while the events were still fresh and the subject matter meaningful.

There is now some doubt about the origin of many prints, especially indigo resists, that were previously thought to be of American manufacture. There is little that was distinctive enough about American design or production in the eighteenth and early nineteenth centuries to make positive identification possible. It was not until the twentieth century that American technology and design made a unique contribution to the field of fabric decoration. Especially significant was the development of screen printing, today widely used by industry and handcraftsmen.

Contemporary Decorated Fabric

Color-decorated fabrics produced by industrial and hand methods are making a vigorous and dynamic contribution to our cultural milieu. The need for patterned surfaces seems to be increasing as a reaction to the post-war Modern style that has been a strong influence since the late 1940's. The clean, precise, and sometimes austere quality of the Modern style is being replaced by or juxtaposed with surfaces that are richly embellished and highly expressive of the individual.

Fabrics, lush in color and surface texture and decorated with a myriad of motifs, are available to enrich the environment. All categories of apparel and commercial and residential interiors make increasing demands upon the producers of decorated fabrics to fill the growing need. When the demand is great, the thought and planning that go into development of the product are frequently minimal. Watered-down copies and quick translations result. There are, however, designers for industry and artist-craftsmen whose concern is with quality in design and execution. The results of their concern provide the illustrative material for this section.

Screen print on linen, by Meda Parker Johnston.

In order to fully appreciate the development of decorated fabrics in our era, a familiarity with the technological advances since 1900 is useful. The screen process method of printing was patented in England in 1907 and about twenty-five years later was successfully adapted to commercial uses. Much of the early work in this technique was limited to printing on paper and felt, the latter used for banners. Since this printing utilized inks or pigments rather than dyes, the fabrics produced were stiff of hand; they were suitable for drapery fabrics but seldom for apparel. Developments in the use of dyes altered this situation after 1940.

Although the procedure of forcing dyes or pigments through a screen stencil has remained basically unchanged, the speed and ease with which it is accomplished have been greatly improved. Where hand methods are employed, procedures for ensuring correct registration and movement of screens and the squeegee have been refined. However, fully automatic screen printing is now widely used by industry. In this method the screens remain stationary while the fabric moves under them, receiving any number of perfectly registered color prints. The printing capacity of these machines ranges from 100 to 400 yards per hour.

Roller printing is still widely used in commercial printing, but the technique has limitations, especially in the size of the repeat. Photographic techniques are now used in place of the old hand methods to transfer a repeat to the roller, greatly reducing the cost of producing a new design.

Prior to World War I most of the commercial dyes available to the American market were produced under European patents. Because they were unavailable during that conflict and again during World War II, American companies were forced to develop a diversity of dyestuffs. As new fibers were developed, too, dyes were required to color them, and at present there are over 1,500 dyes available in this country. In 1956 the fiber-reactive dyestuffs were introduced, providing craftsmen with dyes that produce bright colors of excellent fastness and may be applied with relative ease.

The designs of many of the outstanding decorated fabrics produced commercially and by handcraftsmen seem to have certain characteristics in common. There is a healthy concern for the potentials of the materials and processes of decoration techniques, leading to constant investigation and exploration. Design grows out of the materials and processes in a natural way. Fewer realistic drawings and paintings are imposed upon printing techniques. A freer approach, emphasizing rich color and flowing pattern, is resulting in fabrics which possess unity of design and are suitable for a variety of uses.

A sound relationship is evolving between handcraftsmen and the industries related to fabric decoration. Industry utilizes design ideas developed by craftsmen and adapts them to production methods. Industry also employs craftsmen to develop new concepts relating design to materials and processes. The craftsman, on the other hand, utilizes the technical developments in his own studio work. These interrelationships between creative individual craftsmen and the designing-producing-marketing complex are subtle and intricate. They are, however, necessary for a continued positive growth in the field of fabric decoration.

"Laurels," by Ben Rose Inc., screen print.

"Reflection," by Elenhank Designers Inc., screen print.

"Chinoiserie," designed by Kathleen Johnson for Isabel Scott Fabrics Corp., screen print.

"Horizons," by Berta Wright, screen print on silk.

"Primavera," designed by Don Wight for Jack Lenor Larsen Inc., screen print on cotton velvet.

"Woodland," by Elenhank Designers Inc., screen print.

"Waterlilies," by Jack Lenor Larsen Inc., batik on cotton velvet.

"Leaves," by Sister Mary Remy, brayer print and batik on silk.

"Andante," by Boris Kroll Fabrics, Inc., screen print.

"Luana," designed by Zelda Strecker Thomas for Rowen Inc., screen print.

"Nile Grass," by Elenhank Designers Inc., screen print.

"Landscape," by Jack Lenor Larsen Inc., screen print.

"Floral," by Sister Mary Remy, block print and batik on silk.

"Facets," designed by Jason Harvey for Knoll Associates Inc., screen print, pigment on fiber glass.

"Mira," by Knoll Associates Inc., screen print on linen.

"April," designed by Alexander Girard for Herman Miller Textiles, screen print.

"Discs," designed by Ross Littell for Knoll Associates Inc., screen print, pigment on fiber glass.

"Eden," by Win Anderson Fabrics Division, Jack Lenor Larsen Inc., screen print.

"Bravissimo," by Boris Kroll Fabrics Inc., screen print on cotton velvet.

"Ebb Tide," by Jack Lenor Larsen Inc., batik on cotton velvet.

Tie-discharge and dye on cotton, by Meda Parker Johnston.

"Red Bird," by Sister Mary Remy, block print and batik on silk.

"Batik," by Ruth Adler Schnee, screen print on linen.

2. The Criteria of Design

Good design, like good painting, cooking, architecture, or whatever you like, is a manifestation of the capacity of the human spirit to transcend its limitations. It enriches its maker through the experience of creating, and it can enrich the viewer or user who is equipped to respond to what it has to say.*

Design, in its broadest aspects, affects all phases of our lives today. It is an attitude, not a process or a product. In this volume our primary concern is the relationship of design to the fabric surface in a non-structural way. It is our purpose to encourage the craftsman to reach his own meaningful design solutions by increasing his awareness of his past heritage and his present environment.

It is not our intention to provide a complete experience in basic design in this chapter. We do wish to describe those aspects of design which relate specifically to fabric decoration. The elements of design and the principles by which these elements are applied are basic. Neither of these sets of concepts is the magic answer to good design. Rather, they provide a common basis for discussion and a point of reference. The use of them is not always clear but, more often, they must be subtly interrelated to produce an effective design.

Why decorate fabrics? The answer is a simple one. Decoration serves as a foil to plainness, to relieve the boredom of unembellished surfaces. Though the answer may seem obvious, the solutions to the design problems posed are not. Design for the surface of fabric presents special problems that must be understood if effective results are to be achieved. This does not mean there are ironclad restrictions or few possible solutions.

One unique aspect of fabric surface pattern is that it frequently is not used as designed. The flat, single-plane patterned surface may be draped in an interior or on a human figure, cut up and reassembled in a variety of ways, that is, used on curved surfaces or three-dimensional forms. The surface design is thus distorted from its original state on the single plane. This is the first important principle the designer must realize. A design should work well in a number of situations. Of course, some fabrics can be designed for a specific use, with room for few or no variations. These cases are rare. We see upholstery

*George Nelson, *Problems of Design* (New York, 1957), p. 13.

fabric used effectively for apparel, and dress fabric applied as wall covering. The designer cannot assume responsibility for every use his fabric is put to, but he must realize the possible uses and design with them in mind.

Elements of Design

Line has been described as a series of connected spots and as a moving point. As a moving point it can suggest motion in a variety of ways. A line may be rectilinear or curvilinear, and if it meets itself, it can enclose a space, creating a shape. A line has a very personal quality that grows out of the materials and the individual manipulating them. Each individual and each material has unique qualities that contain great potential for a variety of lines. It is of the utmost importance to fully understand the significance of this potential. Each of the decorating techniques described in later chapters possesses potential for certain unique types of lines or edges. Visualize, for example, the lines created by a knife cutting film, a brush trailing blockout, a gouge moving through linoleum or wood, a cord tightly binding fabric, and a tjanting tracing a flow of hot wax.

Lines possess other qualities which are generalized. Some connote stability, while others suggest movement, agitation, or calmness. Lines can also create optical illusions. The sensitive designer will discover these characteristics and take advantage of their qualities.

A line meeting itself encloses an area which is called a *shape*. A flat silhouette that is either solid or partially filled is also a shape, and it can be either representational or abstract. Using the techniques of fabric decoration, the designer is free to apply a great diversity of shapes to the cloth surface. Some shapes are more readily achieved with one technique than with another. Thus the individual must become familiar with the unique qualities of each medium in order to express his ideas most successfully.

Color is the most complex of the elements of design, and much has been written about it. A number of color systems or theories have been developed, beginning with that of Sir Isaac Newton in the seventeenth century. Systems currently in use are the Ives, Munsell, Otswald, and Prang. All of these have certain terminology in common, while they differ in complexity and means of classification. It is our intention here to give the information necessary for the craftsman to conduct investigations of his own to gain an understanding of the use of color in fabric decoration.

"Lines," designed by Alexander Girard for Herman Miller Textiles, screen print on cotton. A simple use of lines creates a rhythm through repetition.

"Spheres," designed by Ross Littell for Knoll Associates Inc., screen print, pigment on fiber glass. Lines of several weights are used to create complex shapes.

Block print, resist on cotton, India, 20th century. Dots are used to create lines, and some of the dot-lines enclose shapes.

"Feathers," designed by Alexander Girard for Herman Miller Textiles, screen print on cotton and polyester. Shapes creating more shapes by overprinting are used in simple repetition to achieve a flowing pattern.

"Quatrefoil," designed by Alexander Girard for Herman Miller Textiles, screen print on cotton. Surface pattern is achieved by repetition of a basic shape in six colors.

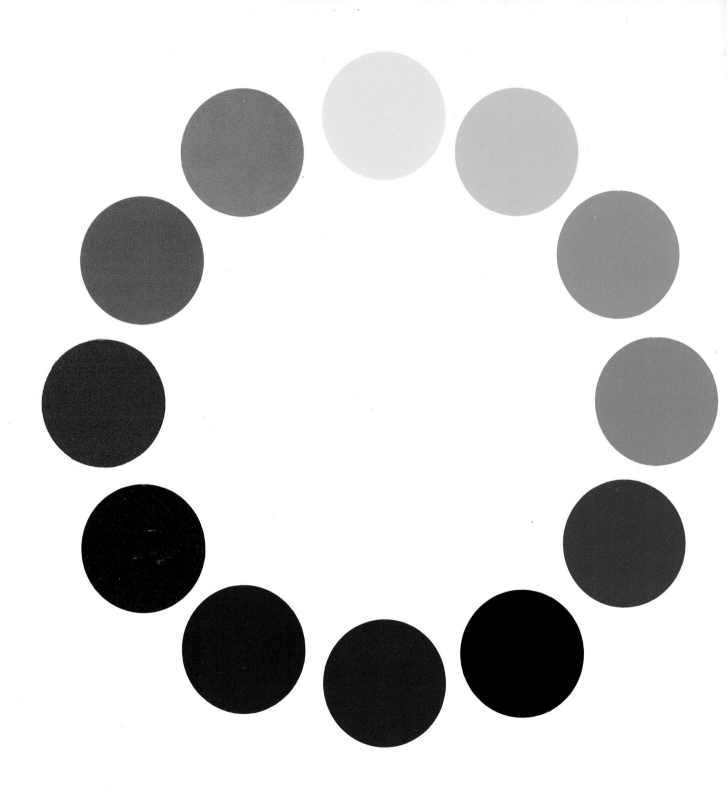

The Prang 12-hue color wheel. Reading clockwise from the top, the hues are: yellow, yellow-green, green, blue-green, blue, blue-violet, violet, red-violet, red, red-orange, orange, and yellow-orange.

The terms used to describe the characteristics of color are hue, value, and intensity (chroma). Hue refers to the basic or pure color. The number of hues in the systems listed above varies from twelve to twenty-four. For purposes of clarity, we shall utilize the Prang system, which is based on three primary hues (yellow, red, and blue), three secondary hues, and six intermediate hues. The secondary hues (orange, violet, and green) are formed by combining each of the primaries with one of the other two. These six hues are placed equidistantly around a circle to form a color wheel. Combining each of the six hues with its neighbor creates the six intermediates (yellow-orange, red-orange, red-violet, blue-violet, blue-green, and yellow-green). The wheel is now complete with twelve basic hues.

Value refers to the lightness or darkness of a color and is designated in terms of the amount of white or black that has been added to it. If white is added to a hue, the resulting color is called a tint and is higher in value than the original hue. If black is added to a hue, the resulting color is called a shade and is lower in value than the original hue. When gray is added to a hue, a tone is created.

It should be noted that when working with dyes, tints or higher values are achieved by extending or weakening the concentration of the color with special extender or water, while when working with pigments, white or an extender is added.

Intensity (chroma) refers to the saturation of a hue in any color. To lower the intensity of a hue, its complement, the color directly across from it on the color wheel, is added. This will tend to gray or neutralize the hue. Intensity is also decreased by any change in value.

The use of color in fabric decoration requires an understanding of the terms defined above and an ability to use the properties which colors possess. Whether the craftsman is using pigments or dyes, the principles are the same (except as indicated above in the section on value). There is obviously wide latitude in mixing colors prior to printing, but unique to fabric decoration is the potential for creating additional colors by means of overprinting. This technique of laying one transparent color over another to create a third on the fabric is readily accomplished with dyes and is possible with pigments if the color has been extended to make it transparent.

Texture involves an interrelationship between the visual and tactile senses. In fabric decoration the craftsman is dealing with a fabric surface which may have strong textural qualities itself. In addition, a visual texture can be added in a variety of ways through the effective contrast of spacing and size of shapes and lines. Each decorating technique will contribute textural effects, since the shapes and lines which make up the texture are the result of

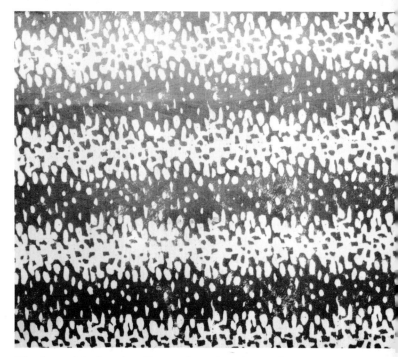

Linoleum-block print. Textured surface is used to create stripes of light and dark.

Tie-dye. Lines and irregular shapes result in a broken, textured surface.

the tools and materials of that particular technique.

Space is illusionary on a two-dimensional surface. It is created by the knowledgeable use of individual elements or a combination of them. The individual characteristics of each of the elements contrasting with the others will suggest spatial relationships. Thus, thick lines may seem to advance and thin lines recede if hue and value are judiciously used to emphasize the illusion. Contrasts of the individual characteristics of shape, texture, and color, too, all can contribute to the illusion of movement in space. It should be noted, however, that the feeling of space may be affected by the use to which the fabric is put. If it is draped, new spatial relationships may result as original ones become altered by light and shadow and distortion of the pattern.

The elements of design described above—line, shape, color, texture, and space—are interrelated in application on the basis of certain principles of design. Again it should be made clear that any terms used in describing approaches to design are not meant to provide rigid formulas or perfect solutions to any problem. They can be useful in analysis of decorated fabrics and in helping the craftsman to achieve more successful results.

Principles of Design

Rhythm is achieved through some form of repetition that creates a feeling of movement or flow on a fabric surface. There are specific ways in which rhythm can be achieved. One is by continuous repetition of a single element or a set combination of them, resulting in an allover pattern. Another is by a progressive change in the unit as it is repeated. This change can be in size, shape, texture, or color.

The principle of rhythm lies at the core of design for fabric decoration because repetition of a motif is inherent in a number of techniques. The repeated pattern which creates a flow over the entire surface, whether it is flat, draped, or covering a three-dimensional form, is of primary concern. It is extremely important that the craftsman have an understanding of the importance of rhythm in design for fabric surfaces. In the succeeding chapters those who are unfamiliar with this principle will have the opportunity to experiment with its application and gain understanding through direct involvement.

While rhythm is a primary concern in the design of fabric surfaces, there are other principles that are useful in developing the repeat, the basic unit of much fabric decoration. If the repeat is thought of as a composed unit which relates to itself, these

"Pebbles," by Ruth Adler Schnee, screen print on linen. Small irregular shapes contrasting with a dark ground give a feeling of texture.

"Primavera," designed by Don Wight for Jack Lenor Larsen Inc., detail of a screen print on cotton velvet. Contrasting values are positioned to give a feeling of space.

Block print, resist on cotton, India, 12th
14th century. Rhythm is created by repetition of a single unit and use of space that is equal to shape. (The Metropolitan Museum of Art, Gift of V. Everit Macy, 1930)

"Haven," by Elenhank Designers Inc., screen print. A feeling of space is created by combining strong dark linear shapes with light broken areas.

"Strings and Things," by Ruth Adler Schnee, two-color screen print on cotton. Rhythm is created by repetition of a basic shape—the circle—that changes in size, value, and spacing.

"Facets," designed by Jason Harvey for Knoll Associates Inc., screen print on fiber glass. This design illustrates symmetrical balance.

Fragment of a resist print on cotton, India, 14th-15th century. Found in Fostat, Egypt. The curvilinear lines create asymmetrical balance. (Courtesy of The Cooper Union Museum)

other guiding factors can be helpful. However, they are useful only if they do not destroy or adversely affect the rhythm of the unit repeated.

Balance is that principle which implies stability. The stability may be real because it is due to an equal arrangement of elements, or it may be illusionary. Symmetry and asymmetry are two qualities that can give balance to a design. Symmetry can be classified as axial when the balance is created along a line or axis by a mirrored image, and as radial when the balanced parts radiate from a central point. A cross is an example of the first type, while a star or sunburst illustrates the second. Asymmetrical balance can be achieved in a variety of ways through imaginative manipulation of the elements of design. The size and number of shapes and their relation to a central point can create a feeling of balance, as can the effective placement of color on a fabric surface.

Emphasis is that aspect of design which creates a focal point or center of interest and brings attention to a specific area. Emphasis, like balance, can be achieved through the well planned use of the elements of design. It can result from lines that direct attention or from the placement of shapes. Color can be an effective tool for creating emphasis. By variation or contrast in hue, value, or intensity, a center of interest can be established. Texture and a greater or lesser degree of detail can have similar results.

The designer should consider the *compatibility* of the various qualities of the basic unit in order to achieve a harmonious result. Flowing brushstrokes are not readily combined with hard-edged, precise geometric shapes in a single repeat. This does not mean that a variety of shapes, lines, or textures cannot be combined in a unit. It does mean that careful thought and planning are required if the allover rhythm of the surface is not to be destroyed by discordant components.

"Windbreak," by Elenhank Designers Inc., screen print. Emphasis is achieved by a contrast of value.

Painted cotton, Peru, ca. 1100-1400. Emphasis is achieved by variation in shape and spacing. (The Textile Museum, Washington, D.C.)

When the elements of design have been combined in such a way that the fabric surface has a satisfying sense of rhythm, the design can be said to possess *unity*. Any final analysis of a particular fabric design, however, must be reserved until the fabric is put to some use. Are the relationships satisfying when it is made into a garment, gathered into drapery folds, covering a wall, chair, or sofa? The answer to these questions will determine whether the specific design exhibits unity.

It should be emphasized that no section of this book will provide instant design inspiration for the craftsman. The survey of historical and contemporary fabric decoration has been included to provide those interested with a background in the evolution of styles and techniques. The challenge, then, is to use techniques and designs which are a reflection of today's world and not to rely on past cultures for easy and quick solutions.

Coupled with a knowledge of the history of fabric decoration, therefore, should be an acute awareness of our present environment, both natural and man-made. We gain knowledge of our environment through meaningful perceptual experiences. In fabric design, the visual and tactile experiences are of greatest importance. If we are interested in expanding the reserve upon which creative design is built, these experiences cannot be left to chance. Perception is a dynamic process in which sensation is related to the individual's accumulated experiences. Increased sensitivity to the environment can lead to a new awareness, and this awareness can have direct results in design for a fabric surface. A walk through a wood in spring may suggest an arrangement of lines, a combination of shapes, or subtle variations in color that, when related to past experiences, can result in sketches, refinements, and, eventually, a fabric print.

Each person is unique in his range and combination of experiences, and since design is related to these experiences, the designs each craftsman creates should also possess a uniqueness which is an expression of the individual. A design for fabric is the result of a unique idea combined with a process that utilizes certain materials. The idea is of first importance, because it brings a sense of unity to all the elements of the design.

3. Planning a Design

The vocabulary of design outlined in the preceding chapter provides a groundwork that will give meaning to experiences with materials and processes. There is no substitute for the understanding gained by direct involvement with the techniques of decorating fabrics.

There are, of course, many ways to approach the design of a fabric surface. One that is emphasized throughout this book is based on an understanding of the potentials of each technique. In order to realize what the potentials are, the craftsman is encouraged to experiment freely with the tools, materials, and processes of each technique to get the feel of its unique qualities. This experimentation may lead to the idea for a specific design or suggest the way in which an existing idea can be realized. The free exploration of the potentials of a technique is not meant to result in any kind of finished design. It should suggest ways of ornamenting a fabric surface with a design and a process that are compatible.

In addition, the craftsman should explore tools, materials, and processes of graphic design that may or may not be directly related to a specific decorating technique. The suggestions for experimentation which follow are intended to give the craftsman a variety of experiences in design. These experiments will result in arrangements of design elements that may be utilized in design for fabrics and that will be a personal expression of the craftsman.

These arrangements, or basic units, may be put into a repeated pattern, and methods for planning a repeat are described below. The use of color, another important consideration in planning a design, is discussed in the final section of the chapter.

Design Experiments

Paper can be manipulated in a number of ways to gain experience with line, shape, and space. It is recommended that color not be a primary concern in the experiments outlined in this section.
(1) Cut a number of identical shapes from folded black paper and arrange them on a grid in a variety of repeated patterns. Glue down the patterns which use the shapes in repetition effectively. Repeat the experiment with strips of black paper which vary in length and width.

(2) Divide a space in either a symmetrical or an asymmetrical way by cutting a rectangle of black paper into pieces. Arrange them on a piece of white paper in the following ways: (a) discard some pieces and use space as an element; (b) use all the pieces and space them equally; (c) use all the pieces and space them unequally. Glue down the effective patterns.

(3) Fold a piece of black paper in halves, quarters, or eighths and cut out a series of shapes. Note the symmetry created both in the cut-out shapes and the remaining skeleton as a result of the folding. Place the skeleton on a piece of white paper and glue it down. On another piece arrange the cut-out shapes in a symmetrical pattern, trying variations in spacing. When a satisfactory pattern is achieved, glue the pieces in place.

(4) Repeat the exercises suggested above with torn paper and study the characteristics resulting from the use of this particular process in contrast to those achieved with cut paper.

(5) Fold or pleat rice paper horizontally, vertically, or diagonally and dip the edges in waterproof ink. Analyze the relationship between the method of folding and the resulting patterns.

(6) Select a small object with a flat side that will print a shape. Corks, spools, blocks of wood, or household objects of plastic can be used. Use tempera, designer's colors, or printer's ink to print the shape in many possible arrangements. Try numerous variations, including patterns of stripes or spots or allover effects.

(7) Use brushes, pens, and sticks with a liquid medium to make lines and shapes. Study the special qualities that result from using each particular tool on various surfaces.

(8) Dip sponges, crumpled paper, plastic, or fabric in liquid media such as paint or ink and experiment with the novel textural effects they give when printed.

(9) Manipulate liquid media by spraying, dribbling, and pouring and study the design potentials of these processes.

Symmetrical design made with folded and cut paper in repeat.

Rice paper folded and dipped in ink.

Design made with torn tissue paper.

Screen print, torn paper used for the stencil.

A variety of arrangements made by stamping a simple shape on paper.

More variations in the arrangement of a shape stamped on paper.

(10) Experiment with traditional drawing techniques using pencil, charcoal, crayon, and pastel. Note the graphic effects created by using these media on different materials: for example, the texture achieved with crayon on a rough surface.

Many of the experiments described above can be duplicated in specific fabric decoration techniques, while others can be adapted to achieve similar results. Design techniques involving cutting can be realized in cut-film screen printing; brushwork can be utilized in screen printing or direct methods. The photographic screen process can duplicate most effects produced with liquid media.

The craftsman may choose to experiment with design media and, after discovering their potentials, seek a decoration technique that will enable him to realize a certain effect on fabric. On the other hand, he may wish to work with a certain decoration technique and seek a design medium which will reproduce the effects on paper for purposes of planning. In either case it is essential to plan the design on paper and analyze it critically before transferring it to fabric.

Textures created by stamping on paper.

Screen print on fold-and-dye ground. The symmetrical cut-paper design was made with a cut-film stencil.

Direct painting with dyes. Brushstroke and wet-on-wet effects are achieved through this direct approach.

Repeats

The repeat is the basic unit of design in the decoration of fabric by printing techniques, and it may also be desirable with direct methods, resists, and tie-dye. Once the basic unit has been established, it must be put into repeat. Repetition of the basic unit should create a rhythmic flow over the whole fabric.

The basic unit may repeat in a number of ways, as illustrated. These examples should be considered as guidelines; the craftsman may arrive at his own variations depending on the technique used and the nature of the basic unit.

There are a number of decisions that must be made concerning the basic unit before it can be put into repeat. One of these is its size, which is influenced by several factors. The technique used determines the maximum size of a single unit. The width of the cloth to be decorated also affects the size of the repeat. Standard widths vary from 36 to 54 inches, and the repeat should be adapted to the fabric selected.

The method of joining one basic unit with the next should also be considered early in repeat planning. There are three ways in which this can be accomplished. In a butt joint the units meet each other along a straight line. This can be used when the unit consists of a series of shapes or lines arranged in rows. In the dovetail joint a portion of one unit fits into a part of the next, without touching it. The overlapping joint, in which the units overlap, can be used when the effect of a continuous line or shape is required. In using this joint, careful thought must be given to effects created by overprinting.

There is an optical device that is helpful in determining whether a design will be satisfactory in repeat before the final adjustments of the unit are made on paper. It requires two mirrors, each big enough to reflect the basic unit. They are placed at right angles to each other, perpendicular to and at one corner of the unit. So placed, the mirrors will reflect the unit in repetition, giving the illusion of a continuous design.

Tracing paper in large sheets or in rolls provides a way to put a unit into repeat. This paper should be used freely to make the first rough layouts and the adjustments of the final repeat. A piece of tracing paper large enough to accommodate at least four repeats is placed over the unit so that the unit occupies one quarter of the paper. Assuming that the internal arrangement of the unit is satisfactory, adjustments are made only at the edges. The outer

Types of repeats.

BLOCK

BRICK

HALF DROPS

DIAMOND

OGEE

58

"Cordwood," by Ruth Adler Schnee, screen print. This design repeat can be achieved by using the butt joint along a straight line.

Screen print, by Win Anderson Fabrics Division, Jack Lenor Larsen Inc. This illustrates the kind of design repeat that can be achieved with the dovetail joint.

"Windflower," by Jack Lenor Larsen Inc., screen print. The overlapping joint is utilized in this kind of allover, continuous pattern.

edges of the unit are traced with a soft pencil. Now the paper is moved so that the unit is directly above or below the one just traced. The way in which the two units join should be studied, and the spaces occurring between the units should be analyzed in relation to the spaces within the unit. The spaces created will be an integral part of the total design and must be carefully considered. The type of joint to be used should be decided upon, and adjustments are now made to accomplish this.

Butt joints are frequently simple to achieve; however, exact registration in the printing process is imperative. Dovetail joints also require adjustments at this time. With the tracing paper over the unit, the elements are traced in existing positions only where the joining is satisfactory. Where adjustments are necessary, the outlines of elements in new positions are drawn in. For clarity these changes may be drawn in another color pencil. It is advisable to try several variations on tracing paper to ensure the best possible solution. When adjustments for top and bottom have been made, the tracing paper is shifted so that side adjustments can be made in a similar manner. As a final check, the unit should be repeated four times, so that all joinings can be seen, analyzed, and adjusted.

The overlapping joint is frequently the most difficult one to achieve. A color overlapping itself will usually create a darker value, an additional element in the design. The overlap should be considered part of the design and carefully planned or creatively utilized. Its effect may be minimized by careful study of the unit in repeat and selection of the points where overlapping will take place. Narrow shapes, lines, and textures frequently provide the ideal point of joining. The procedure is the same as for dovetail joints, with adjustments made where necessary. A completed drawing that shows the unit joined on all sides will allow the craftsman to determine whether the pattern is unified.

Color

It is possible to plan a design almost to finality without the introduction of color. Each craftsman develops the method of planning best suited to his experience and goals. Some work with color from the beginning, while others prefer to introduce color after a unit is in repeat. However, the craftsman is inevitably faced with decisions about using colors in combination. There are a number of generally agreed upon characteristics which can be used as guides for combining colors. Knowledge of them

may prove helpful to those whose experience with color has been limited. These characteristics fall into two broad categories: those involving related hues and those involving contrasting hues.

Monochromatic colors are derived from one hue; however, a great deal of variety can be achieved by changes in value and intensity. *Analogous* colors are those with one hue in common, such as yellow, green, and blue-green (yellow is the common hue). Colors related by hue are placed in two groups: those related to red are referred to as warm colors, and those related to blue are referred to as cool colors. Generally speaking, warm colors advance and cool ones recede.

Complementary hues are two that lie opposite each other on the color wheel. When they are mixed together, the intensity is lowered, and gray can result. Studies in the physiology of color vision indicate that the same receptors in the retina of the eye are sensitive to complementary colors. Thus, when complementary colors are juxtaposed in certain ways, they tend to reinforce each other. The effect can be one of strong optical vibrations and agitated movement. Judiciously used, for example in points of emphasis, complements can subtly enhance each other. *Split-complement* refers to the combination of a color with the hues on either side of its complement. Orange used with blue-violet and blue-green would be considered a split-complement. A *triad* is a combination that includes any three hues which are equidistant on the color wheel. Orange, green, and violet form a triad. The combination of hues in a triad results in a dominance of either warm or cool colors.

In developing a design it is important to simulate as closely as possible the final effect a dye or pigment will give to a fabric surface. There are several liquid media which resemble dyes when thoughtfully used. Waterproof ink is transparent, and it is readily available for experimenting with color effects. Felt-tipped markers are also readily available and provide another source of transparent color with effects similar to those of dyes. Fabric dyes can also be used for design development on paper by making a small amount of dye into a paste and adding water to achieve the proper intensity of color.

The craftsman may wish to start working with the three primary colors and proceed to more complex relationships. A transparent color can be brushed on paper, allowed to dry, and overlapped with others to experiment with the effect of overprinting. The inks can be lightened by thinning with

Screen print and batik on cotton velvet, by Meda Parker Johnston. Three colors—turquoise, blue-violet, and golden yellow—result in a multicolored fabric through the effective use of overprinting with fiber-reactive dyes.

Color-sample grid printed in fiber-reactive dyes. All formulas used are full-strength colors.

Color-sample grid printed in fiber-reactive dyes with full-strength and extended colors.

water and mixed to achieve other colors. The purpose of such exercises is to learn something about the nature of transparent color, and no attempt should be made to create an organized design.

Tempera and designer's colors can be used to simulate the effects created by pigments on fabric. The craftsman may wish to execute some of his work with pigments. Although many effects are possible with them, they have less potential for fabric decoration than dyes.

It is beneficial to execute some sample work with the actual dyes or pigments. To observe the changes in value and intensity that result from overprinting, a series of rectangles or other shapes can be printed in some arrangement, such as a grid, on properly prepared fabric (see Chapter 4 for directions for preparation of the fabric). A good way to experiment is to print a number of sample grids using full-strength and reduced colors in various combinations. Starting with formulas of full-strength

dye or pigment, a series may be printed as follows: full-strength paste, 1 part paste to 1 part extender, 1 part paste to 4 parts extender, and 1 part paste to 10 parts extender. It is important to keep an accurate record of this work and file it for future reference.

When a multicolor design results from printing a separate unit for each color, each color in the rendering can be traced separately to provide a cartoon for preparation of a screen or block. This is called color separation. The separation may be done with tracing paper. Allowances should be made for joining and registration. The original design should have a registration mark (a small cross) that will be matched on each color separation and on the printing device (as described in Chapter 4). Designs with two or more colors are not always the result of this separation, however, but may result from varied placement of a single screen or other printing device.

A basic unit put into repeat on tracing paper.

A four-color separation on tracing paper that provides cartoons for stencil-making.

4. General Considerations

The information given in this chapter is basic to the techniques of fabric decoration. It is essential for the craftsman to be familiar with the general characteristics of fabrics and media and the processes of pretreatment, fixation, and finishing in order to obtain satisfactory results with any technique. The craftsman who wishes to use printing techniques must be familiar with the general procedures for preparation of the printing table and registration.

Materials and Equipment

Some equipment is necessary for the planning and execution of all fabric decoration, while there are some materials which are useful and may be acquired gradually by the craftsman. A detailed list of the specific materials required for the various techniques is given at the beginning of each chapter. However, a brief summary of commonly needed equipment is provided here for the convenience of the craftsman. Of course, not all of the items listed are necessary to begin decorating fabrics: they are included to indicate the type of supplies the craftsman will wish to collect.

The work area should be provided with or located near a source of water. Sinks are needed for dyeing and washing, though washtubs can be substituted for them, and a hose with a spray nozzle is an added convenience. A table which can be padded for printing purposes (as described below) will also serve as a work table if it is protected with a cover of muslin or plastic sheeting.

A stove or hot plate, a steam cabinet or improvised substitute (also described below), and a steam iron are necessary appliances for many processes and techniques, and an electric kitchen mixer and fan are useful. A clothesline and plastic clothespins are used for drying fabric.

Scales which will weigh up to 600 grams (about 1½ pounds) and an immersion thermometer, such as a candy thermometer, are needed for work with decorating media. Deep pans or tubs of stainless steel, enamel, or plastic, and assorted mixing bowls of the same materials are used for dyebaths and mixing dye pastes, as are measuring spoons and a cup with 1-ounce markings.

The usual studio equipment for planning designs includes a drawing board, construction paper, newsprint, sketchpads, tracing paper, and watercolor and rice paper, as well as scissors and a variety of artist's brushes and sponges. Drawing inks, felt-tipped marking pens, watercolors, designer's colors, tempera, pastels, and wax crayons are among the media that may be used in designing. Small but especially necessary items are a staple gun, 1-inch masking tape, T pins, pushpins, and thumbtacks.

A yardstick, ruler, and metal measuring tape are needed, and a good supply of newspaper, absorbent rags, non-absorbent cardboard cut into smooth-edged, small pieces, glass jars with lids, and tin cans should be collected for various purposes. A light table or box is required for preparing photographic stencils in screen printing, and it is a convenience for transferring designs onto fabric (a dressmaker's carbon and tracing wheel may also be used for this purpose). A light table can be improvised by placing a piece of plate glass over upright supports and clamping a light underneath.

Finally, a supply of a kitchen cleanser of the abrasive type, household bleach, color remover, waterproof glue, mineral spirits, turpentine, benzene, spar varnish and solvent, and shellac and solvent should be kept on hand in the studio.

Fabrics

The following section on Media explains in detail the possible combinations of fabrics and decorating media. In general, the most successful fabric decoration using dyestuffs, with the materials and equipment available to the average craftsman, will be achieved on the natural fibers: cotton, linen, silk, and wool. Viscose rayon is the one man-made fiber that is especially recommended. (Methods for identifying the various types of fibers are given in Chapter X.) Cotton and linen which have been mercerized have greater affinity for dyes because of the chemicals used in the mercerizing process. A wider range of fabrics can be utilized when pigments are the media used for decoration. These media can be applied to the man-made fibers and blends as well as to all the natural ones. Very inexpensive fabrics are good for experimenting with repeats and design ideas, but they give unsatisfactory results when decorated with some dyes.

Fabrics to be decorated can be sheer or closely woven, and their surface textured or plain. These individual characteristics may inspire designs, or a fabric with certain characteristics may be chosen because it is appropriate for the spirit of a preconceived design. The choice of weight and texture is also influenced by the final use of the fabric, whether for upholstery, drapery, pillows, wall hangings, apparel, etc.

Media

Detailed and technical reference information for the preparation and use of fabric decorating media is given in Chapter 10. However, the craftsman must be familiar with the types of media that can be used in the techniques of fabric decoration and with their characteristics, which will influence the choice of an appropriate medium, and this information is summarized here.

The various techniques of fabric decoration require various methods of color application. In block printing, screen printing, and painting, color is applied in pastes. Resist techniques require cold baths of color, and tie-dyeing can be done in either hot or cold baths. The craftsman may choose either dyes or pigments to make pastes, while only dyes can be used for color baths.

The difference between the two types of media, dyes and pigments, may be explained in simplified fashion by comparing the substances with which they are mixed to make a paste and the way they act on fabric. When a paste is made with a dyestuff, the color is dissolved in water with the aid of chemicals known as assistants, and a special thickening material is added to achieve the desired consistency. When the color is applied to the fabric and fixed, it forms a bond with the fiber. Pigments, in contrast, are made into paste by suspending them in a binder. When the color is applied and fixed, the pigment lies on top of and around the fiber instead of penetrating it.

Dyestuffs are divided into groups or classes. They vary in their method of application, their brilliance of color and fastness to washing and light, their affinity for the various fibers, and their ability to withstand aftertreatments involving boiling. There are many classes of dyestuffs, but only those most useful to the individual craftsman are described here.

Acid dyes can be applied in pastes and in hot baths. They are brilliant in color and available in a wide range of colors, from which the most light- and washfast may be chosen. They are especially suitable for wool, silk, and some synthetics, but lack affinity for cellulosic fibers. They will not withstand boiling.

Basic dyes can be applied in pastes and in hot or cold baths. They possess remarkable brilliance, but in general have only poor to moderately good washfastness and poor lightfastness, so they are useful for articles which will only be exposed to artificial light. They have a natural affinity for silk and wool. They will color cotton, linen, and viscose rayon, for which the use of a mordant is required. They will not withstand boiling.

Direct dyes can be applied in pastes, in hot baths, and, in some circumstances, in cold baths. Many colors lack brilliance and general fastness. They may be overdyed with basic dyes for brilliance. They have a natural affinity for cotton, linen, and viscose rayon. Some also dye silk and wool, where wash-fastness is usually better. They will not withstand boiling.

Disperse dyes can be applied in pastes and in hot baths. They are brilliant in color and have moderate to good fastness to washing and light. They are especially suitable for synthetic fibers and will also dye silk and wool. They will not withstand boiling.

Fiber-reactive dyes can be applied in pastes and in cold baths. They have exceptional brilliance and fastness to washing and light. They are suitable for cotton, linen, viscose rayon, and silk. They will withstand boiling.

Household dyes can be applied in pastes and in hot baths. They generally are not brilliant in color, but they are light- and washfast. They are direct dyes and are suitable for all the fibers dyed with this class of dyestuffs. They will not withstand boiling.

Prepared vat dyes can be applied in pastes. The brilliance of the colors varies. They are light- and washfast. They are suitable for cotton, linen, viscose rayon, and silk. They will withstand boiling.

Soluble vat dyes can be applied in pastes and in cold baths. They are brilliant in color and very fast to washing and light. They are suitable for cotton, linen, and viscose rayon. They will withstand boiling.

Mineral colors (ferrous sulfate and permanganate of potash) can be applied in cold baths. They produce earth colors and are light- and washfast. They are suitable for cotton, linen, viscose rayon, and silk. They will withstand boiling.

Pigments are generally brilliant in color and have relatively good fastness to light and washing. They can be easily applied to most fibers, except wool, by printing and some direct methods. The range of colors available is more limited than that of dyes. Most are sold as pastes that require little preparation prior to use. Each manufacturer supplies specific information on fastness and directions for use which the craftsman should follow for reliable results. Textile pigments may be classified according to the binder in which the ingredients are dissolved or suspended.

Emulsion pigments are the most widely used group and are available from a number of manufacturers. Most are based on oil or synthetic resin and water which, with some brands, is used as thinner and solvent for clean-up.

Synthetic-base pigments use synthetic oil or resin as a binder and are thinned and cleaned up with solvents such as mineral spirits.

Oil-based pigments employ a natural oil as a binder. Printer's inks can be used satisfactorily for block printing and some direct methods, but are not suitable for screen printing.

Pigments are easy to apply and fix without special equipment. They can be used for both opaque or transparent color, in contrast to dyes, which are always transparent. However, the disadvantages of using pigments are that they obscure the natural qualities of the fiber and do not seem a part of the fabric because they lie on the surface. Fabrics decorated with pigments also are slightly stiff of hand.

It is sometimes desirable to achieve a light-colored design on a dark ground. Pigment pastes can be used to print a light color on a dark ground if they are sufficiently opaque. With dyestuffs there are two general methods for obtaining this effect: by discharging existing color and by resisting color. The discharge method can be used with any of the decorating techniques by starting with a colored fabric and applying a bleaching substance to remove the color in the design areas. In the resist method, design areas of a light ground are reserved or protected with some substance which will resist dark color applied over it. (This process is the basis of batik and related techniques of decoration, and tie-dyeing also utilizes a form of resist.)

Pretreatment of Fabric

Any fabric to be decorated with any medium must be washed free of sizing with warm water and mild soap, thoroughly rinsed, and dried. Some types of fabric need ironing after they are washed, while others will stretch out wrinkle-free when pinned to the work table.

A fabric which has been treated to resist wrinkles, soil, or water will not accept the decorating medium properly. Such permanent finishes can be removed by treating the fabric in a bath of ½ ounce hydrochloric acid per 2 gallons of water at 190°F. for 30 minutes, followed by a thorough rinse and a detergent bath to remove all traces of the acid from the fabric.

Some media require that the fabric be further prepared before decorating by washing in a special formula which is vital to the success of the colors. The manufacturers of the media will supply directions for their products, and it is important to follow them for satisfactory results.

Fixation of Decorated Fabric

Almost without exception the media used in fabric decoration require fixation—the process by which the medium is permanently fixed in or attached to the fiber. It has been noted that some media have a higher degree of fastness than others.

All fixation processes are basically treatments with heat. Dyestuffs applied in pastes and in cold baths almost always require steam treatments. (Dyestuffs applied in hot baths are fixed in the dyeing process.) The procedures described here are for the fixation of printed, painted, or cold-dyed fabrics (unless otherwise specified in Chapter 10).

After a fabric has been decorated with a dye paste, most of the dyestuff is held in the dried film of the thickening agent: very little will have penetrated the fibers. Steaming causes the printed areas to absorb moisture, forming very concentrated dyebaths in which penetration of the fiber by the dye takes place. Under correct steaming conditions the thickening agent prevents the dyestuffs from migrating or spreading outside the printed area. However, if the steam is too moist or the dye paste was improperly mixed, the film of thickener becomes so diluted that migration occurs. If the steam is too dry or the dye paste contained too much thickener, insufficient moisture is absorbed, and the dyestuff does not fix properly; much of it may wash away in the finishing process.

Very simple equipment may be used to steam the dye-decorated fabric. The illustration on page 68 shows how an enamel preserving kettle can be used. Enough water is placed in the kettle to last an hour at boiling temperature. The rack which usually holds bottles or jars is turned upside down to serve as a shelf. Precautions must be taken to protect the fabric from accidental wetting, such as that from condensation on the sides and top of the kettle or spattering of the boiling water. Any spotting with water will cause unsightly bleeding in the printed areas. A layer of felt is placed on the shelf for this purpose, and several layers of newsprint over it provide further protection. Neither the felt nor the paper should touch the sides of the kettle.

A layer of newsprint or thin cloth is laid on a table, and the decorated fabric is placed over it. The two are rolled together from end to end and then made into a coil with a string tied around it. This package is placed on the shelf with more paper and felt on top of it. Nothing should touch the sides of the kettle. The water should be boiling when the coil is placed in the kettle. The fabric should remain in the covered steamer for at least an hour. To ensure an even penetration of steam, the package of fabric should be removed, opened, rerolled from the other end, and tied up again. More water is added to the kettle, if necessary, and the fabric is steamed for another hour. The coil must be untied and unrolled immediately upon removal from the steamer. A large pressure cooker can be used in the same way as the kettle if a shelf is improvised.

The type and width of fabric are factors that must be considered when the use of an improvised steamer is planned. A 3-yard length of very fine batiste will make a comparatively small coil, while a 3-yard length of wide sail cloth will be much more bulky.

A steam cabinet can be built out of plywood and lined with galvanized metal. The interior should be sprayed with a rust preventative. The peaked roof eliminates the possibility of dripping caused by condensation. The steam is provided from below by water heated with immersion heaters, and perforations at the top of the cabinet ensure a flow of steam through the fabric. The quantity of steam required depends on the volume of the steamer. Approximately 1 quart of water should be converted to steam per hour for each cubic foot capacity of the steamer. (A 1-kilowatt heater converts about 1½ quarts of water into steam per hour per cubic foot.)

The metal rack shown in the illustration of a steam cabinet on page 69 was made using a drawer slide for the side rails. Holes in the rack hold hooks to which the cloth is fastened. (T pins can be bent into hooks for this purpose.) The holes are set 2 inches apart to keep the fabric from touching itself, and the rack is placed so that there are 2 inches between the hanging fabric and the sides and ends of the cabinet.

A thermometer is inserted in one of the perforations in the top to give the inside temperature of the cabinet. The cloth is entered at about 200°F. It is advisable to have it already placed on the rack and to open the door, let out the first burst of steam, and then place the rack on the track and close the door as quickly as possible. It will be noticed that

LID

FELT

PAPER

WRAPPED
FABRIC

PAPER

FELT

RACK

PRESERVING
KETTLE

WATER
LEVEL

IMPROVISED STEAMER

STEAM CABINET

A   HOLES FOR ESCAPING STEAM

B   SLIDING RACK TO HOLD FABRIC

C   EXPANDED METAL SHELF

D   WATER LEVEL

E   HEATERS

the temperature is greatly lowered for a moment, but it will rise to 200°F. quickly as the water continues to boil.

The length of time the fabric must be steamed varies with the nature of the fiber, the weight of the fabric, the type of dyestuff, and the steaming equipment. The craftsman should experiment to find the time required for the best results. An efficient steamer with very hot, circulating steam requires less time than one which must reheat after the fabric is entered. The preserving kettle heats faster and to a higher temperature than the steam cabinet. However, the kettle holds less fabric, and there is more danger of spotting from condensation. Because the fabric is tightly folded in the kettle, more time is required for adequate penetration by the steam.

Most dyestuffs, such as the basic, direct, and acid dyes, need about an hour of steaming time. The fiber-reactive dyes can be steamed this long, but 30 minutes is usually adequate for a medium-weight fabric. Heavy fabrics such as velveteen and certain linens and cottons may require an hour, while sheer fabrics may need only 5 or 10 minutes.

Pigments are fixed in a number of ways. Most require the application of heat to become permanently attached to the fabric. Fixation results from evaporation, oxidation, polymerization, or a combination of these. In evaporation, the solvents pass into the air as gas, leaving the pigment dry on the fabric. Oxidation is a chemical process in which ingredients combine with oxygen in the air to form new compounds. Polymerization is also a chemical action in which the molecules of pigment form larger molecules that adhere to the fabric.

The fabric is usually air-dried as recommended by the manufacturer and then ironed on the reverse side for 5 minutes with a hand iron set for cotton. If the fiber will not stand this high temperature without injury, the setting can be lower, and the fabric ironed for a longer time. Some craftsmen use a bank of lights which is attached above the table in such a way that it can be passed over the fabric to heat one section at a time. The fabric may also be placed in a laundry dryer for about 30 minutes with the heat set at high temperature. Fabrics decorated with pigments can also be fixed by steaming if the temperature is high enough. (The manufacturer of the pigment will specify the temperature and time required for heat treatment.)

Fabrics printed with printer's ink should be air-dried for 5 days, then dipped in a bath of 1 teaspoon of vinegar per quart of lukewarm water, dried partially, and ironed while still damp from the bath. Some brands of pigments do not require any treatment for fixation other than air-drying. Experiments based on the directions supplied by the manufacturer will show whether the proper combination of fiber, paste, and fixation process is being used.

Finishing

Fabrics decorated with dye pastes and in cold dye-baths require washing as a finishing process after fixation in order to remove excess dye, chemicals, and thickeners. The kind of washing—from gentle, cool baths to vigorous, boiling ones—depends on the tenacity of the thickener and the resistance of the specific dyestuff to washing and boiling. Washing will remove the thickener, which causes the fabric to be stiff, and a slight brightening of colors will usually be noted.

It is not necessary to finish the fabric immediately after steaming. However, once the finishing operation is started, it should be completed. The fabric is rinsed in cold water until all the loose dye is removed. (The finishing process will vary slightly depending on the dyestuff used. Additional treatments for each class of dyestuff are specified in Chapter 10.) It is very important not to let the fabric sit in water colored with the loose dye. The fabric is hung up to dry partially. Ironing it at this point is easier than dampening it again after it has dried thoroughly.

The craftsman should refer to the directions supplied by the manufacturer concerning finishing of fabrics decorated with pigments. Fabrics decorated with pastes containing a thickener should be washed in a detergent bath, rinsed, and dried. Most pigments, however, require no finishing. For future cleaning needs, dry cleaning is usually recommended, though most of the media will withstand gentle washing.

Preparation for Printing Techniques

Some preliminary preparation is required for the printing techniques of fabric decoration. It is much more satisfactory to attach an entire piece of cloth to a surface for printing repeated designs than to work on small sections of the fabric and move it. Some designs may be too closely repeated to achieve perfect alignment after repinning the fabric to the work table.

The size of a printing table will depend on the kind of printing the craftsman wishes to do. How-

PRINTING TABLE

A MASKING TAPE

B T-PINS

C FABRIC TO BE PRINTED

D MUSLIN BACK CLOTH

E MUSLIN COVER CLOTH

F $3/8''$ FELT UNDERPADDING

G PLYWOOD TABLE TOP

ever, printing is usually done on yardage (3 yards or more of fabric). A table that is constructed especially for printing, therefore, should be more than 3 yards long to allow for several inches extra. It should also be at least 6 inches wider than the fabric to be printed; if space permits, a 60-inch-wide table will allow printing of all standard widths of cloth. A top of plywood, ½ to 1 inch thick, should be reinforced with 1- x 2-inch pine stock. Permanent legs of wood or metal may be attached; a height of about 30 inches is convenient. When studio space does not accommodate a table of these dimensions, the top can be set on sawhorses of the proper height, and the table dismantled when not in use. If the table is permanent, shelves can be built between the legs for screen storage. An ideal arrangement is vertical dividers that hold the screens in an upright position.

If the table surface is resilient and will give a little under the pressure of color application, more perfect color coverage can be obtained. A layer of felt or rug padding is tacked to the table top, a layer of muslin is stapled over it, and a back cloth of muslin is pinned over both with T pins. The back cloth is fastened tightly and straight with the table; the pins are placed with the bar on the selvage and the point directed toward the center of the cloth, piercing the padding. The back cloth is a temporary base for printing. It is removed and washed after each use because the dyes often penetrate through the fabric being printed to the padding beneath. During printing the wet areas are likely to pick up any dry dye left in the back cloth.

The fabric to be printed can be pinned in place on the work table, or if the padding is protected with a waterproof cover, it may be adhered to the surface with gum. However, since some dyes, such as the fiber-reactives recommended here, do not react favorably with the gum, the pinning method is preferred.

A measuring stick is used for a guide to mark a straight line across one end and along one side of the table with a soft pencil. The fabric to be decorated is attached with T pins starting at the side. It is pulled, stretched, and pinned until the entire side is fastened on the penciled line. To avoid scallops along the sides, the pins should be about 1 inch apart. The end of the fabric is pinned against the penciled line, and care should be taken not to stretch it out of shape at this point. The second side and end are then pinned by pulling the fabric straight from the opposite sides. Some adjustment of the ends is always necessary to take care of the fullness which

results from stretching. Pinning the cloth straight and tight will help ensure a print on the straight of the cloth and will reduce registration problems caused by the tendency of the fabric to expand when wet and contract upon drying.

Some provision must be made for correct registration, or exact repetition, of block printed or screen printed designs. A very heavy T square, made of at least 2- x 6-inch pine stock, provides a simple tool to aid in the proper placement of the block or screen. Matching marks on the T square, table, and blocks or screen frames are referred to as registration guides.

To prepare for correct registration, a continuous strip of masking tape is placed over the pins along one selvage. Another strip is taped over the edge and along the bar of the T square. The dry block or screen is laid on one corner of the fabric so that it is adjacent to the taped selvage. The first horizontal row of prints will be here. The T square is placed above the block or screen, with the head fitted tightly against the table and the block or screen firmly in place against the bar. A pen or pencil mark drawn on the selvage tape where the edge of the T square rests across it will indicate where to place the T square when the first row of the design is printed. (It should be noted that the registration marks for the T square are placed only on one side of the table.) A small piece of tape is placed on the back of the block or on the frame of the screen on the side touching the T square. Another mark on this piece of tape matched to one on the bar will be the guide for the first print of each row.

It will be realized that registration guides for the length of the cloth will be placed on the selvage tape, and those for guiding the printing across the width of the fabric will be matched to the marks on the blocks or screen frames and the T square. To determine the placement of marks on the bar for the second and following prints across the cloth, the width of the design on the block or screen is measured. To this figure is added any space to be left between prints. This sum is the distance to be measured and marked on the bar from the first mark and at succeeding intervals across the fabric. The mark on the block or screen will be matched to each of these as the printing proceeds across the fabric. To guide in printing the following rows, the measurement of the length of the design plus the space to be left between prints is the sum used to measure from the first mark on the selvage tape for the second and following rows to the end of the cloth. During print-

Top view of printing table and screen, showing the use of adjustable stops for registration.

ing, the T square is moved to each of these as needed.

A second method of registration which is commonly used for screen printing is that of the guide rail with adjustable stops. This requires screens the width of the fabric. A metal guide rail is aligned with and attached to one side of the table. Sliding stops with locking devices are attached to the rail.

The distance between the stops is adjusted to the length of the repeat of each individual design, and the stops are locked into position. Screws are attached to the side of the screen, resting against the guide rail. These can be moved in or out to further adjust registration and guide the frame in coming to rest against the stops.

5. Block Printing

Materials and Equipment

Artist's Spatula
Brayer
Flock
Linoleum-cutting Tools and Sharpening Stone
Linseed Oil
Pad for Paste
Plate Glass
Plywood
Sandpaper
Saws and Drills (hand or power)
Sieve
Unmounted Linoleum
White Paint or Shoe Polish

Many materials and devices have been used for printing fabrics. One of the earliest techniques may have been dipping leaves and twigs in some color substance and pressing them on fabric. There is evidence of the use of incised bamboo, clay in the form of tablets and rollers, copper strips imbedded in wood backing, and, probably the most popular through the ages, the wood block. Linoleum has replaced the wood block for many craftsmen in the West. However, cardboard, plastic, rubber, cork, metal, and an endless list of other materials, either man-made or natural, may create decoration on fabrics. When dyes, paints, or inks are applied to the surface of a block and the block is stamped on cloth, a print results.

Design Potentials of the Technique

The unique qualities of the linoleum-block print will be realized if the craftsman takes advantage of the special characteristics of the material. In linoleum-block printing the shape of the cutting tools combined with the resistance of the material produces a typical "mark of the tool" unlike that of any other material. Practice on scrap linoleum will give a familiarity with this inherent characteristic of the technique, and the craftsman will soon find that ideas for prints develop from his experiments. The sharp, definite edges offer possibilities for numerous variations. Such effects as softly changing edges and values should be left for some other tools and materials to produce.

The cut-wood block offers a simple, direct approach to fabric printing utilizing readily available materials. Saw-cut wood shapes with plain edges and surfaces can be used to create interesting designs if attention is given to size, shape, and grouping. To experiment with the possibilities, a piece of paper may be cut and reassembled into a motif. A piece of wood of the same dimensions is cut and assembled in the same manner and glued to a backing to make a block for printing. Design is governed in some degree by the tools used for cutting the wood. The many possibilities for arranging the motif in repeat will become apparent with experimentation on paper or inexpensive fabric.

A variety of existing objects can be used for print-

Details of block prints showing the mark
of the tool.

ing with little or no alteration. Great potential lies in odd bits of metal, plastic, and wood, as well as numerous types of plant life. The challenge of printing with found objects is in arranging them in such a way that they lose their individual identity and create a design.

The hard surfaces of most printing blocks resist dyes, creating textural effects in the print. This may be considered a design potential rather than a limitation. A solid effect can be created by flocking, which gives the block an absorbent surface. Additional textural effects can be created by using weathered wood or some other material with an uneven surface.

Found objects and the resulting prints.

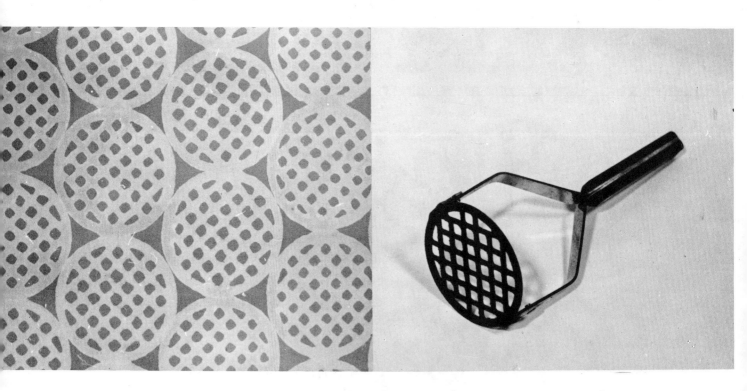

Preparation

WOOD. The size of the printing block and, consequently, the size of the motif are limited by the manageability of the block in the printing process. A small motif can be repeated more than once on a single block to reduce the number of times the block must be stamped. It is difficult to apply color evenly to blocks larger than 12 inches square.

Shapes for wood blocks can be cut from plywood ⅜ to 1 inch thick or from solid wood at least ⅜ inch thick. A variety of handsaws are available which can be used for cutting the block, depending on the shapes required. When cutting by hand, the wood can be held in a vise. If power tools are available, blocks can be cut with circular, band, or jigsaws, and additional effects can be achieved with drills and other woodworking tools. Normal safety precautions should be exercised in working with all cutting tools.

In block printing the motif is reversed when printed; consequently a design should be reversed before tracing it on the wood. Tracing paper is convenient for reversing the motif because it can be turned over and the motif traced on the back. Soft pencil rubbed over the front of the drawing will serve as a carbon for transferring the design onto the block.

A rectangle of paper cut and rearranged to form a basic unit.

The shapes traced on plywood.

The completed cut-wood block.

Prints on fabric showing variations in placement. Textured areas result from unflocked shapes, solid areas from flocked ones.

77

Some shapes are more manageable if glued to a ¼-inch plywood backing. When several shapes are printed as a motif, it is essential to glue them to a backing. A waterproof glue is recommended, and the manufacturer's directions should be followed. One side of the backing should be straight, giving an edge to locate against the guiding mechanism used. The backing may extend beyond the motif to form hand holds, or handles may be glued or nailed to the back of the block.

To prevent the block from absorbing water, dyes, and pigments, it is necessary to cover all surfaces with two coats of shellac. When dyes are used, the shellacked surface will give an uneven print or textural effect. For an even, solid print the block should be flocked. Flock is a finely shredded fiber which, when adhered to the block, gives it an absorbent surface. A special adhesive is available to hold the flock, although the waterproof varnish called spar varnish works very well. This is poured or brushed thickly over a flat, non-absorbent surface such as glass or a piece of Masonite, and the block is stamped onto it, thus picking up the varnish only on the printing surface. Flock is then sifted very thickly over the surface, and a piece of cardboard or wood is pressed over the flocked area to achieve better adhesion. It is left to dry for several hours before the excess is shaken off. A more absorbent surface is achieved with two or more applications of varnish and flock.

LINOLEUM.   To make a linoleum block, a piece of linoleum the size of the motif is mounted on a piece of plywood at least ⅜ inch thick. Large sheets of linoleum can be mounted on plywood, and a complete block can be cut the size required. The backing

Cutting a linoleum block against a bolt head.

of the linoleum block should be shellacked in order to protect it from water, dyes, and pigments.

Before transferring the motif to the linoleum, the linoleum should be lightly sanded with fine sandpaper to remove its waxlike surface. The block is then coated with a light-colored, water-based wall paint or white shoe polish so that the design can be seen easily. The motif must be reversed before it is traced on the block in the same way as for the wood block. The block is now ready to cut.

Most studio accidents are caused by dull tools and the improper handling of tools. Linoleum knives are relatively inexpensive and should be replaced often. A sharpening stone should be a part of carving equipment. Whatever cutting tools are used, the fingers should be kept behind the blade at all times. A dull tool tends to slide, and a painful cut can be suffered if a finger is in front of the knife. For ease of cutting, a large bolt can be dropped into a hole in the work table. The bolt will turn as the block is shifted against the head. If the linoleum is difficult to cut with well sharpened tools, it may be heated slightly in an oven or other heat source.

Linoleum, like the shellacked wood surface, gives an uneven print or textural effect when dyes are used. For an even, solid print the block can be flocked in the same manner as the wood block. Shallow depressions and narrow lines or spaces between shapes may need to be cleaned out with the linoleum tools after flocking. This should be done after the adhesive and flocking have dried completely.

In all block printing, guides for registration must be indicated with marks on the back of the block for matching with those on the T square (described in Chapter 4).

Flocking a linoleum block.

Printing Procedures

The printing procedure varies depending on the printing medium used. In all cases some kind of pad on which to spread the dye or pigment is necessary. For dyes and most pigments, a pad consisting of a piece of ¾-inch plywood, double the dimensions of the block, is covered with a piece of resilient material such as rug padding or felt cut slightly smaller than the plywood. This surface is then covered with a heavy-duty plastic film which is held by staples or tacks on the reverse side, and over this a piece of thin felt or other absorbent fabric is fastened.

The dye should be the consistency of honey, and it is applied evenly to the surface of the pad with a 2-inch brush. The block is then stamped onto the dye-coated pad a number of times in several positions until the surface is evenly coated with the dye, but not so heavily as to fill up small depressions. The block is properly positioned on the fabric and firm pressure is applied evenly to all areas with the hands. Experimentation with small samples of the fabric will indicate the amount of pressure needed to achieve an even print. It may also be necessary to

Step-by-step procedure for linoleum-block printing with dye paste.

vary the consistency of the dye or the amount of dye on the pad. When several acceptable trial prints are achieved, printing of the actual fabric may begin. It is essential to achieve a consistent application of dye to avoid dark and light areas in the finished print.

When printing with pigments, the color is mixed with the extender provided by the manufacturer and thinned to brushing consistency with a recommended thinner. The surface of the pad is then coated evenly with ink using a 2-inch brush. The block is stamped onto the pad as described above. Several trial prints should be made, varying the

pressure applied and the consistency of the pigment paste as needed, before proceeding with the work.

There are oil-based printer's inks which may also be used for block printing on fabrics. These inks are spread on a piece of glass with a metal spatula and rolled out evenly with a rubber or gelatin brayer. The brayer picks up an even coat of ink, which is then rolled onto the block. If the ink is too thick, it may be thinned with a few drops of linseed oil. Inking the block with several light coats is preferable to one heavy coating. The printing is the same as for dyes and other pigments.

Applying pigment to felt-covered pad for block printing.

Applying textile printer's ink to a linoleum block.

Blocks may be printed with printer's ink on acetate film, enabling the craftsman to reproduce the characteristics of block prints photographically. (The section on photographic stencils in Chapter 6 should be referred to for the procedure.)

Linoleum-block prints.

Clean-Up

When dyes are used, cleaning blocks and equipment is easily accomplished with water, sponge, and a stiff brush. Solvents such as mineral spirits or turpentine should be used with pigments. A convenient method for cleaning blocks and brayers is to soak them in a large, deep cake pan containing the solvent. Depressions in the blocks may be cleaned with a stiff brush, and the equipment should be dried with a soft cloth.

6. Screen Printing

Materials and Equipment

Absorbent Cotton
Acetate Film
Adhering Liquid
Bakelite Squeegee or Direct Emulsion Coater
Brown Paper Tape (3-inch)
Brushes (soft)
Caustic Resist Enamel
Cutting Tools for Film
Developer
Developing Trays
Film Remover
Frames for Screens
Glycerin
Inks (opaque and waterproof)
Lamp (photoflood or carbon arc)
LePage's Glue
Liquid Wax Resist
Photo Emulsion
Plate Glass (¼-inch thick)
Presensitized Photo-stencil Film
Rubber-based Liquid Blockout (Maskoid)
Sandpaper
Sensitizer (ammonium dichromate)
Squeegees
Stencil Fabric
Stencil Film
Stove Enamel
Tusche

Screen printing is the most recently developed of the fabric decorating techniques. It grows directly out of the Chinese stencil print. In stencil printing the design is cut in a sheet of cardboard, specially prepared paper, plastic, thin metal, or wood, and the dye is applied to the fabric through the cut-out areas. Screen printing works on the same principle, but the screen holds all the parts of the stencil together, and the printing medium is pulled across all the openings with one stroke, forcing color onto the fabric.

The technique has many advantages over the older methods of printing fabrics. It is much less laborious, because the size of the design or the number of repeats may be much larger than is possible with other methods, and once the design is on the screen, it may be saved and reused indefinitely. It has advantages for design because sharper and more intricate detail can be reproduced than with other techniques. With photographic screens it is possible to reproduce any graphic art work.

Design Potentials of the Technique

Since screen printing is based on the stencil technique, its design potentials will be evident upon examination of the various ways in which the stencil may be created on the screen. Each of the methods described below for blocking out some areas while leaving others open possesses special characteristics. Design ideas may result from these characteristics; on the other hand, certain designs suggest the use of specific stencil materials. The craftsman should become thoroughly familiar with the various stencil materials or blockouts that are available and with the solvents used to remove them. He can then plan to use them singly or in combination. The first decision must be which printing medium to use.

Stencil materials must be those which are not destroyed by the printing medium or its solvent.

Preparation

FRAMES AND SCREENS.   If a ready-made frame is not used, one can be constructed. The most popular wood for making the frame that holds the screen is kiln-dried white pine, but spruce, mahogany, basswood, and boxwood are sometimes used. The important consideration is that the wood be as knot-free and as well dried as possible. For frames with outside dimensions up to about 15 x 20 inches, 1½- x 2-inch stock may be used. As the frames increase in size, the stock must become proportionately larger. A 20- x 30-inch frame should be made of 2- x 2-inch stock, and one measuring 30 x 40 inches requires at least 2- x 3-inch stock. Frames made of wood which is too thin will warp more quickly and drastically from the pull of the stencil cloth, from cleaning with water, and from general use and storage.

Several types of joints may be used in the construction of the frame. The frame must be rigid and have smooth edges and surfaces. Large frames should have metal corner plates for reinforcement.

A specially woven silk is commonly used for covering the frame, though in some cases cotton organdy, nylon, Dacron, or vinyon may be used. However, a good stencil silk, thoroughly cleaned after each printing and carefully stored, will last indefinitely. Domestic or Swiss screen process silks are available, and they are numbered, with XX following the numeral. The numerals denote the size of the mesh (the larger the number, the finer the mesh), and the X's the strength of the weave. (All silks used in the processes described here are XX weave.) For printing on fabric with pigments, 8XX or 10XX is recommended; for printing with dyes, 10XX or 12XX is suggested. It is convenient to identify indelibly on each finished screen the mesh size of the silk used.

Silks may be purchased in widths from 40 to 80 inches. It is economical to figure the most advantageous width for the size of the frame to be covered. Leftover pieces should be saved for covering small color-testing frames.

There are several methods for attaching the silk to the wood frame. It is most commonly done with tacks or staples, the groove-and-cleat, or the groove-and-cord. The last two methods require special equipment, and the beginner will find that stapling is adequate and the staple gun easy to manage without help. The objective is to have the silk as tight as a drum head and free from soft spots and ridges. It is helpful not to cut the required amount of silk away from the whole piece until the frame is covered, so that finger holds are available.

The silk is placed over the frame so that the selvage is parallel with a side and is about ½ inch inside the outer edge of the frame. Several staples are used to tack the silk to one corner. Next, the silk is pulled taut and straight and stapled at the next corner. Then the entire side between the corners is fastened, the staples placed about 1 inch apart and on a diagonal. Another corner is stapled after the silk is pulled taut and parallel with the edge; then the entire side is fastened. The silk is stapled to the remaining corner and sides in the same way. A second row of staples is placed around the entire frame, staggered between those of the first row and slanted in the opposite direction. Any staples which are not flush with the wood are hammered down, and the excess fabric is cut away.

The silk should be washed to remove any soil or size. A kitchen cleanser is especially suitable because the abrasive powder will slightly roughen the surface of the silk, preparing it to adhere more satisfactorily to the stencil.

Brown paper tape 3 inches wide is used to protect the wood and fabric and to keep the printing medium from seeping out between them. Two strips of the tape, 2 inches longer than the length of the outside of the frame, and two strips, 2 inches longer than the width, are cut. They are creased by folding down the center, glue side in. Each strip is dampened with a sponge and placed on the frame so that half of the tape is over the staples and silk, and the other half is over the outside wood edge of the frame. The tape is smoothed and helped to adhere by rubbing with a dry cloth. The tape which extends

Adhering paper tape to the exterior edges of the frame.

Screen print on cotton velvet, by Toshiko Horiuchi. This four-color print was done with a cut-film stencil utilizing the overlapping joint.

beyond the corners is snipped along the crease and folded flat against the wood.

The frame is turned over, and corner pieces are made. Four squares of the tape are cut and folded in half in both directions; then one crease is snipped just to the center of each square. When one quadrant with a cut edge is folded over the other, the square will fit into a corner of the frame, making a protective seal.

More tape is cut, creased, and glued along the interior edges of the frame so that it adheres to both silk and wood. One or two strips of uncreased tape should be adhered across the silk on the two shorter ends of the frame, on both the inside and outside of the screen. This provides a reservoir for the printing medium that is 3 to 6 inches wide at each end. The wider reservoir is necessary for a large frame.

When the tape is thoroughly dry, all paper and wood surfaces are waterproofed with several coats of shellac or lacquer-proof blockout. The thick liquid is pulled across the paper and wood with a stiff piece of cardboard held perpendicular to the surface. The blockout should extend about ¼ inch onto the silk.

Registration guides are now established on the screen. With the frame silk side up, a fine-tipped pen, waterproof ink, and a T square are used to draw centered horizontal and vertical lines that extend from edge to edge. If the silk is properly stretched and light pressure is used, there is no danger of damaging the silk. These lines will ensure proper placement of the design on the silk and aid in correct registration. Of course, registration guides must be marked on the frame to match with those on the T square (described in Chapter 6).

SQUEEGEES. The squeegee is the instrument used to force the ink or dye through the stencil onto the fabric being printed. It is a tool with a wood handle holding a blade of synthetic rubber. It should be an inch or two shorter than the inside of the frame it is used with, so that the entire width of the design is

88

printed in one stroke. Several squeegees of varying widths, therefore, may be needed.

The handle of the squeegee should not be too large for comfortable use with one hand. If the edges are sharp, they should be sanded, and the handle should be shellacked to protect it during washing. The better squeegees have screws holding the blade in place. If there is an open space between the blade and the handle, printing inks will collect there and create problems in cleaning the tool.

It is very important to purchase squeegees which are made especially for textile printing. They have thinner and more flexible blades than those used for printing on paper.

When the blade of the squeegee is dull, uneven, or nicked, it will deposit an uneven amount of ink in printing. It may be sharpened with fine sandpaper, emery, or garnet cloth. These may be purchased in long strips or by the yard from screen process sup-

ply houses. The abrasive is fastened to a wood base, perpendicular to which an upright piece is attached. The squeegee is held against the upright so that a straight edge will result, and it is drawn back and forth until the edge is smooth and sharp again.

To avoid the inconvenience of having the squeegee fall into the ink between strokes, it is recommended that nails or small dowels be driven into the ends of the wood handle. These will rest on the frame and keep the squeegee upright when the printer releases it between strokes.

Stencils

Stencil materials may be divided into two general categories: those which may be used with dye pastes and those which may be used with pigments. The following tables list stencil materials which may be used as permanent and temporary blockouts and the solvents for them.

Printing Media	Permanent Blockout Stencil Material	Stencil Remover
Dye pastes	Lacquer-based knife-cut film	Lacquer thinner
	Lacquer-based liquid blockout	Lacquer thinner
	Lacquer-proof liquid blockout	Remover recommended by the manufacturer
	Photo emulsion on nylon (with caustic resist enamel)	Remover recommended by the manufacturer
	Photographic film on nylon (with caustic resist enamel)	Remover recommended by the manufacturer
	Plastic liquid blockout	Remover recommended by the manufacturer
Pigment pastes	Glue	Water
	Lacquer-based knife-cut film	Lacquer thinner
	Lacquer-based liquid blockout	Lacquer thinner
	Lacquer-proof liquid blockout	Remover recommended by the manufacturer
	Photo emulsion	Water with household bleach
	Photographic film	Water with enzymes
	Plastic liquid blockout	Remover recommended by the manufacturer
	Water-soluble knife-cut film	Water
	Water-soluble liquid blockout	Water

Temporary Blockout Stencil Material	Stencil Remover
Glue	Water
Lacquer-based liquid blockout	Lacquer thinner
Lacquer-proof liquid blockout	Remover recommended by the manufacturer
Liquid wax emulsion	Mineral spirits or turpentine
Plastic liquid blockout	Remover recommended by the manufacturer
Rubber-based liquid blockout	Peel or rub off
Stove enamel	Mineral spirits or turpentine
Tusche (liquid and crayon)	Remover recommended by the manufacturer
Water-soluble liquid blockout	Water

KNIFE-CUT FILM STENCILS. There are a number of films available for various printing requirements. All films are laminated to a thin backing sheet of paper or plastic which holds all the parts of the design not peeled away until they can be adhered to the screen. Plastic backing is preferable because it is more transparent and moisture-resistant than the paper backing. A film which shrinks or expands in damp working conditions can interfere with correct registration.

Good, sharp stencil knives can be purchased in a variety of sizes and prices. Handles are usually about the size of writing tools. Blades can be re-sharpened and used indefinitely. Some tools may be returned to the manufacturer for sharpening when their shape makes it difficult for the craftsman to do it himself. Knives should be kept in good working condition and protected from damage when not in use.

There are special tools for cutting lines of various

Screen prints made with cut-film stencils.

Removing the film from the backing.

widths which strip away the film in the cutting. Other line cutters have two blades, which are adjustable, to cut parallel lines. There are compass cutters for cutting circles and swivel knives for irregular shapes.

In the knife-cut film stencil (lacquer-type or water-soluble), the areas to be printed are cut in the film and peeled away. The film, with the remaining design, is adhered to the screen, and when the backing is peeled away, a stencil is produced. The craftsman should not begin to plan the design on paper until he has gained some understanding of the characteristics of knife-cut film. To discover what these are, a piece of film may be taped to a drawing board, and whatever tools are available used to experiment. The textural effects possible and the variety of shapes, edges, and lines will be evident upon spontaneous exploration of the material and the cutting tools.

When a design has been thoroughly planned on paper and the repeat worked out, it is taped to a drawing board or other flat surface. A piece of film about 2 inches larger than the drawing is cut and placed over it and secured with tape. The film (not the backing) is cut with light strokes, as if the design were being traced. Heavy pressure is not needed and will only drive the edges of the film down into the backing, making it much more difficult to adhere it to the screen. If a white line is

discernible on the underside of the backing, the pressure is too heavy. When the parts to be printed have been outlined, they may be peeled away by lifting an edge or corner with the tip of the knife. A corner with a clean angle rather than a torn one will result if the lines are extended slightly beyond the intersecting point. If the design has very large open areas, small slits should be cut in the backing to provide air vents and prevent buckling during adhering.

To adhere lacquer-type film to the screen, the screen is prepared by wiping it lightly with adhering liquid. The film is laid on a thick piece of cardboard which is larger than the film but smaller than the inside of the frame. The screen is then laid over the film, silk side down, and whatever marks have been used on design, film, and screen to achieve perfect registration in printing are matched. The cardboard will push the film tightly against the silk, ensuring adhesion.

A small wad of cotton is wet with the adhering liquid until it is very wet but not dripping. The screen frame is kept tightly pressed down with one hand, and one stroke is made across a narrow end of the film with the wet cotton. It should be dried immediately by fanning and then rubbing lightly with a dry cloth. Another wet stroke is made, slightly overlapping the first, and dried in the same way.

This process should be repeated until the entire film is adhered. The wet strokes should all be made in the same direction. Light spots show that not enough liquid has been used. These should be repaired after the whole film has been adhered, rather than soaking them with an immediate reapplication. Rubbing too heavily over a very wet area may melt the edges of the film, as will a surplus of liquid left too long before drying.

To adhere a water-soluble film, the screen is prepared by washing with a kitchen cleanser to remove any oil. The cut-film stencil is placed over a thick piece of cardboard which is larger than the film but smaller than the inside of the frame. The moist screen is then laid over the film, silk side down, and registration marks are matched. The screen is kept firmly pressed over the stencil, and a piece of cotton or clean rag soaked with water is used to wet thoroughly and quickly an area of about 10 square inches at one end of the stencil. The stencil is immediately blotted with paper towels, using a slight pressure. Wetting and blotting is continued until the entire stencil is adhered.

When the entire film has been adhered, the screen is set aside to dry for at least 30 minutes, and longer if possible. The backing sheet is removed by lifting one corner and slowly pulling it diagonally away from the film. It may also be removed by pulling from all corners toward the center. It is necessary to watch for any bits of the film which may pull away with the backing. To repair these, the backing is laid in place, and the screen is replaced on the cardboard pad. The process of dampening and drying is repeated over that small area.

After the film is adhered, any silk between the film and the edges of the frame is masked with a liquid blockout. Applying the thick liquid to the screen is best accomplished with a piece of very stiff cardboard, since application with a brush can leave a thick and uneven deposit on the screen. This should always be avoided because any uneven surface will cause the squeegee to lift and leave a poor print around the raised area. The frame is stood on a table and held at about a 45-degree angle. A small amount of the blockout is poured inside the frame in one corner and drawn upward over the silk with the cardboard, which is held perpendicular to the screen, so that a thin layer of blockout is deposited. This is continued from each corner until all the silk is covered.

To remove lacquer-type film from the screen, several layers of newspaper are placed on the work

Screen prints made with cut-film stencils.

table, and the underside of the screen is saturated with the remover recommended for the film used. The screen is then turned over quickly and set down so the film is in contact with the paper. More remover is poured inside to cover the entire area. Paper may also be placed inside the screen over the film. After a few minutes, the paper is removed from underneath and inside. Most of the film should come away with the paper, but the procedure may be repeated if necessary. For final cleaning the screen is stood on its side and held under the arm. Two cloths saturated with remover are used to rub over the silk on both sides of the screen simultaneously. This should remove all traces of the film. The blockout is removed with the recommended solvent in the same manner, and the screen is ready for the next stencil.

Water-soluble film is removed by soaking in water which contains a small amount of vinegar. When it begins to dissolve, it can be removed completely with a brush and warm water.

LIQUID BLOCKOUT STENCILS. The principle of the liquid blockout stencil is that a liquid called a blockout is used to fill in, or mask out, all areas of the screen through which the printing medium is not to pass. The design areas are either left open or are subsequently opened up to permit the passage of the printing medium. The simplest stencil is that which uses a single blockout, leaving the design areas open. However, a combination of two or more blockouts presents greater flexibility of application and thereby broadens the design potentials. The wide choice of liquid blockouts and tools for their application encourages an experimental investigation into the possibilities of this approach to screen printing.

The commercial liquid blockouts available from screen process supply houses fall into four general categories: lacquer-based, lacquer-proof, water-soluble, and a plastic type. All of these may be used with pigment pastes; all but the water-soluble may be used with dye pastes. Thus, the printing medium will determine the choice of blockouts. Each of the blockouts requires its own particular solvent for removal from the screen. Usually the solvent will also serve as a thinner. All blockouts should be kept tightly sealed, as they thicken rapidly through evaporation. In the water-soluble blockouts it is especially noticeable that various brands differ in viscosity. Some are similar to liquid clay; others have a sticky consistency. The craftsman will wish to experiment with a variety of blockouts to discover

Screen prints made with liquid blockout stencils.

what potentials each possesses for design. They can be applied with brush, cardboard spatula, sponge, syringe, or any number of other tools, or they may be dribbled, dripped, stamped, or spattered on the screen.

When liquid blockouts are used to reproduce a design, it is convenient to lay the screen over the drawing and trace it on the silk with a soft lead pencil.

A single commercial blockout is sufficient to make stencils for printing any number of colors with only one screen. The design and printing can be planned to take advantage of the overprinting of colors. When the design is traced on the screen and the registration marks are indicated, the blockout is applied with a brush or some other tool to all parts of the screen except those which are to be printed with the first color. After printing the screen is cleaned, and the blockout is removed completely. The blockout is then applied to all parts of the screen except those which are to be printed with the second color. Some areas of the first color may be left open for overprinting with the second. The second color is now printed. The screen is cleaned, and the blockout removed. The blockout is applied to all parts of the screen except those which are to be printed with the third color. Experimentation will show how many colors can be overprinted successfully.

The disadvantage of the single screen, single blockout method is that the stencils are removed each time, and only one printing of the particular design is possible. The same effect can be achieved by preparing as many screens as there are colors in the design.

Two blockouts may be used together, providing they require different solvents for removal. One serves to temporarily hold the design areas where the printing medium will pass through the screen during printing. It is applied to the inside of the screen, and two coats may be required to prevent the permanent blockout from attaching itself to the mesh in these printing areas. When it is well dried, the permanent blockout is applied, also to the inside, over the whole screen, with a piece of cardboard (as described above). This layer should be as thin as possible, yet fill the mesh completely. The thinness of the permanent blockout makes it more easily removable from the areas to be printed. This is accomplished by saturating the screen on both sides with the solvent for the temporary blockout and loosening the blockout with rags and stiff

brushes. The permanent blockout will come away from the areas to be printed along with the temporary blockout. It is recommended that both sides of the screen be rubbed simultaneously. The screen is now ready for printing.

The craftsman will realize that it is possible to use more than two blockouts on one screen if the succession of their removal is planned so that the solvent for one will not affect those left in the screen. It is a useful method when only one screen is available for a multicolor design. However, it should not be attempted until tests have been made to establish how the various solvents will affect the various blockout media.

The first consideration is the permanent blockout which will resist all the other solvents. For example, the lacquer-proof blockout is not removable with water or the solvent for the plastic type, and most brands are not affected by the solvent for the lacquer-based blockout, so it can be chosen for a permanent blockout. The permanent blockout may be applied to some parts of the design area to hold the ground color of the fabric throughout, adding to the number of colors in the completed print.

After the distribution of colors in the design is decided upon, a water-soluble blockout is applied to those areas where the first color is to be printed. The lacquer-based blockout is then applied to the areas where the second color is desired, and the plastic type to the remainder of the areas to be printed. The permanent blockout is spread over the entire screen. When it is dry, the water-soluble blockout is removed, and the first color is printed. After the screen is washed and dried, the permanent blockout can be used to mask out the areas just printed to reserve that color. If the permanent blockout is applied to only a portion of these areas, additional colors will be created by overprinting. The lacquer-based blockout can now be removed, and the second color is printed. Again the areas just printed are masked out with the permanent blockout, and the plastic blockout is removed from the remaining areas. The third color is printed. Three colors have now been printed; with overprinting and some of the ground color retained, it will be apparent that eight or more colors can be attained with only three printing operations.

The advantage of this method is that a multicolor print is possible, and registration is more certain with only the one screen. A disadvantage is the slowness of the whole printing operation because the work on the screen is carried on between printings.

Another disadvantage is that the stencils for each color are removed from the screen after the color is printed; thus the design cannot be printed again with those stencils. For this reason the craftsman may prefer to have a screen for each color prepared in advance. The resulting design will be the same, and the same print may be repeated as often as required.

A different stencil medium may be used for each screen for the various colors. The unique character of each type of stencil makes it possible to obtain a variety of effects. For example, one stencil may be cut film, which gives a sharp outline, the second may be lacquer-type blockout showing brushstroke effects, while the third may be plastic blockout applied with a sponge, creating textured effects. It should be noted that the standard film used for the knife-cut film stencil is lacquer-based and dissolved by the solvent for lacquer-based blockout, so these two cannot be used in combination. The water-soluble film, similarly, may be used in combination with all but water-soluble blockouts.

Several other materials can be used in place of or in combination with the commercial liquid blockouts. LePage's glue, thinned to 1 part water and 1 part glue, with a little glycerin added, will serve as a blockout that is removed with water. (It should be noted that this is not the household mucilage, but a glue which is packaged in cans and sold at hardware and art supply stores.)

LePage's glue is often used as the permanent blockout in combination with liquid waxes such as tusche or the wax emulsion used by ceramists for glazing. It is usually a wise precaution to apply two coats of the liquid wax, because it is thin in consistency. Solid waxes in the form of soft crayons and pencils add to the design potentials of the wax-glue combination. A popular way of using them is to lay the screen over a raised textured or patterned surface and firmly rub the crayon or pencil over the silk so that the effect of the raised surface is transferred to the silk. Glue is pulled over the entire screen, and the wax is washed away with its solvent and the help of a stiff brush. It should be repeated that the thinnest possible layer of the permanent blockout that still closes all the mesh of the screen is most desirable. Heavy deposits make the removal of the temporary blockout a tedious process.

The liquid waxes can also be used in combination with lacquer-based blockouts but are more difficult to remove than when used with glue.

Some rubber-based liquids (such as Maskoid) are manufactured for use as temporary blockouts. When dry, the permanent blockout is applied, and the rubber is removed by peeling and rubbing it away. It is recommended that the lacquer-based blockout be used as the permanent one with this temporary blockout.

Stove enamel can also be used as a temporary blockout. Though slow to dry, it is a thin liquid which is easily removed from the screen.

For short printing runs or for non-repeat designs, the craftsman will discover other stencil materials. Masking tape can be used to block out areas or to make a pattern. Cut or torn paper will stand up under a few printings with dye pastes and last for many more with pigment pastes. Pale-colored wax crayons can be used to draw on the silk, and the design left there for the duration of the printing, if dye pastes are used. (Dark-colored crayons are apt to stain the fabric.) Pigment pastes will dissolve the wax in the screen. It is also possible to lay thin flat objects or materials in place on the fabric to print over instead of attaching them to the screen. When the technique of screen printing is thoroughly understood, the liberties that can be taken with the materials become more evident.

PHOTOGRAPHIC STENCILS. The photographic stencil makes possible the use of designs with fine detail and other characteristics which cannot be reproduced easily, if at all, with any other stencil. It is much faster to prepare than other stencils and is more accurate, durable, and dependable.

Two types of photographic stencil are available to the fabric printer. One is a film which consists of a gelatin emulsion over a paper base. The other is the gelatin emulsion in liquid form. Stencils made with either of these are suitable for printing with pigment pastes. Since both are soluble in water, they must be specially treated for use with dye pastes.

The basic principle of the process is that when graphic art work done in opaque ink on a transparent surface is placed between a sensitized film or emulsion-covered area and a light source, the areas protected by the ink will remain soft and removable with water, while those which receive light are hardened and will not dissolve in water. The printing medium will pass through the washed-out areas.

The positive, or design to be printed, is applied to a thin transparent material such as paper or plastic which will not buckle when the ink is applied to it. The material most often selected is cellulose acetate, which is available in several thicknesses. Some acetates have one perfectly smooth side and one slightly grained, which will accept pencil sketching that can be erased without leaving a trace. The drawing must be done with an opaque ink which is easily manipulated with pen or brush, does not build up to a thick layer or chip off the plastic surface, and is absolutely light-resistant. These materials are available from screen process supply houses as well as from those who sell industrial art supplies.

There are many ways to prepare a design for the photographic screen. In addition to brushing and drawing on the transparent sheet, an opaque medium can be applied by spraying, spattering, or stamping. Printer's ink can be used for the last. Opaque flat objects can be arranged under plate glass as a positive to produce the stencil. Some obvious ones are cut or torn paper, natural materials such as grasses, leaves, and seeds, and manufactured objects such as string, lace, etc. Other techniques of fabric decoration may be reproduced. Pelon can be tie-dyed with opaque ink and the resulting design reproduced. The possibilities are as varied as the individual imagination.

PHOTO EMULSION STENCILS. Since it is difficult, if not impossible, to remove some of the materials used for the photo emulsion stencil from the screen fabric, it is advisable to use Dacron instead of silk. A 12XX mesh is a good choice, since it should be as fine as possible but still permit a good print with dye pastes. Dacron is much less expensive than silk and resists many solvents and chemicals which will harm silk.

Each manufacturer will supply directions for the use of his product. However, the basic steps for preparing the photo emulsion stencil are as follows:

The screen is scrubbed lightly but thoroughly with a kitchen cleanser. The emulsion and sensitizer (ammonium dichromate) are prepared according to the directions, in a room darkened as recommended. The frame is then laid on the table, fabric side up. Emulsion is poured evenly over the tape at one end and pulled acros the mesh and off the other end of the screen. The tool used may be handmade or one sold for this purpose (called a direct emulsion coater). The tool is wiped dry, and an additional stroke is made, leaving a thin, even coat. The emulsion-coated screen is allowed to dry.

The method of exposing the sensitized screen will depend on the equipment available to the craftsman. It may be exposed with fluorescent, photoflood, or carbon arc lights. It can be arranged so that exposure is from above with an overhead light, or a

Screen print on vinyl, by Robert Kidd. The marbled effect was achieved with a photographic stencil.

Screen print on vinyl, by Robert Kidd. The batik effect was achieved with a photographic stencil.

Screen print made with a photographic stencil. Grasses and other plants were used for the positive.

light table can be used so exposure is from below the screen. A very simple arrangement is the use of a photoflood lamp as an overhead light. The distance from the light source to the frame should be not less than twice the diagonal of the image. This will ensure proper exposure of the whole design area.

In any arrangement, perfect contact between the acetate positive and the sensitized screen is an inflexible requirement. The emulsion-covered screen is placed over a thick piece of cardboard that is larger than the design but smaller than the frame. This will help ensure close contact. The positive is positioned face up inside the frame, and a sheet of plate glass ¼ to ⅜ inch thick is placed over it.

The light is turned on, and the screen is exposed for the time recommended by the manufacturer. This may be from 3 to 30 minutes. Since the strength of light varies considerably, the craftsman should make several tests for the best results. A small screen should be available for experimentation. If the emulsion is underexposed, it will not harden properly and much of it will wash away in the developing, leaving only a thin, pinholed layer on the fabric. If it is overexposed, the light will creep under the opaque ink and harden design areas, preventing them from opening up when the screen is washed.

The exposed screen is removed to a container of water or is placed under the water tap, where water at the recommended temperature will remove the unexposed portions. Both sides of the screen are wet, and a spray or brush can be used to clear the design areas.

The developed screen is laid on newspapers, and the excess water is blotted with more paper. When placed in an upright position, the screen will dry quickly.

A blockout is used to fill the open areas between printing areas and frame if the emulsion was not spread over the whole screen. An occasional pinhole may be found and filled with a water-resistant liquid blockout.

Screens which are to be used with water-soluble printing media must be reinforced with caustic resist enamel, which will prevent the chemical action of the dyes on the emulsion. The enamel is applied with a piece of cardboard. A thin layer is pulled over the inside of the screen, and while it is still wet, the design areas are opened up by rubbing on the reverse side with a soft cloth dampened with mineral spirits. When the screen is thoroughly dry, the process is repeated, but the enamel is applied to the

outside of the screen, and the design is opened up from the inside.

The emulsion may be removed from the screen by soaking it in a mild solution of bleach. When it has been reinforced with the enamel, however, there is little chance of complete removal.

PHOTOGRAPHIC FILM STENCILS. The photographic film stencil makes use of a presensitized film over a plastic backing sheet. Many brands of film are available, each with its own developer, but the procedure followed is more or less the same for all. Elaborate facilities are not necessary for the use of these materials. Each manufacturer will give detailed instructions for his product; however, the general procedure is as follows:

The design is transferred to acetate with opaque ink, and the screen is prepared by scrubbing with a kitchen cleanser. The developer is prepared according to the manufacturer's directions.

A piece of the presensitized film is cut at least 2 inches larger than the design on all sides. Many films may be taken from their tubes only in semi-darkened rooms. The remaining film should be wrapped up and returned to the tube before any bright light is turned on. The film is placed backing side up on a flat surface, and the acetate positive, also with the backing side up, is positioned over it. A sheet of plate glass ¼ to ⅜ inch thick is placed over them.

The exposure time depends on several factors, including the kind of light used and its distance away from the film. These are matters for experimentation. A light table may also be used to expose the film.

After the film is exposed, it is developed in the prepared tray of developer. The film is immersed quickly, film side up. It should be kept in motion under the surface for the time directed by the manufacturer. It is then transferred to a tray of water at the recommended temperature. The soluble areas will wash away. Some manufacturers recommend the use of a gentle spray of water to loosen the soluble parts, while others suggest a soft brush. When all design areas are open, the film is set by placing it in a tray or sink of cold water.

The film is removed from the water and placed film side up on a piece of cardboard which is larger than the design but smaller than the screen frame. This will ensure proper contact. The screen is dampened with a sponge and water and positioned over the film to match registration marks, and they are pressed together lightly. The screen is blotted gently with newsprint until all the moisture is removed.

The film should be allowed to dry thoroughly. Then one corner of the plastic backing is lifted and gently pulled away from the stencil. If there is too much resistance, more time should be allowed for drying. Any open areas around the film are filled in with a liquid blockout.

Printing Procedures

Preliminary tests of the printing medium should be made for correctness of color and consistency. Small screens and a matching squeegee for testing colors should be available. It is also important to have extra fabric for experimenting with color plans.

The order of printing should be planned in advance. To avoid picking up wet color on the underside of the screen frame, which is always much larger than the design being printed, the printing is not carried out in continuous order. It is usual to print the first, third, and fifth positions, etc. of the first row; then, skipping the second row and moving the T square used for registration to the mark for the third row, to print the first, third, and fifth posi-

Process of screen printing showing the alternating placement of the screen.

tions, etc. This alternation is continued to the end of the fabric. Then the second, fourth, and sixth positions, etc. of the second row are printed; the T square is moved to the fourth row, and so on to the end of the fabric until all of the first color has been printed. The same procedure is followed for all the colors, and the same registration guides are used throughout.

Before printing is begun on the fabric, the screen should be "wet-out" by printing it several times on a piece of spare fabric or absorbent paper in order to see that the dye is passing through the mesh properly. The screen is positioned over a sample piece, the squeegee is held 2 or 3 inches from the end of the screen in the area reserved for the printing medium, and a layer of the medium is poured across the screen between the upright squeegee and the frame. The squeegee will prevent the medium from flowing over into the design areas. The screen is held in place with one hand, and the squeegee is placed behind the printing medium and pulled across the silk with a firm stroke. Streamers of the medium should not be left behind. A good sweep of the squeegee should leave the screen with a clean surface. The printer should experiment in advance to find the number of strokes suitable and the proper pressure for the type of fabric being printed.

Position of squeegee for adding printing paste. The squeegee is held and pulled across the screen in the same position.

Dyes print more successfully with the squeegee held at about a 45-degree angle, while pigments require the squeegee to be held in a more upright position. A rapid stroke with light pressure usually results in less printing medium being deposited. This may be preferred for some fabrics, such as thin silk. An evenly distributed pressure as the squeegee is pulled across the screen and the correct angle for the type of medium being used are necessary for achieving a level, well defined print. When this has been achieved, the first color run may begin.

The printing can be done in two ways. With the screen placed lengthwise on the table, the printer can pull one stroke, move to the other end of the frame, and pull the squeegee toward himself again. Another technique is to sweep the first stroke to the right with a backhand stroke and pull it back to the left.

After each print, the screen is lifted by raising one edge and peeling it away from the fabric. It should never be lifted straight up. To avoid smudges from the fingertips, which often pick up color in handling the squeegee, the wood handle should be wiped and the fingers cleaned often.

If it is unavoidable to interrupt the printing operation, the screen should be left where last printed. This will keep the mesh damp and unclogged for a short time.

After each printing, the fabric is left to dry thoroughly before another color is printed. This will prevent blurred edges where overprints occur. A fan may be used to speed the drying.

Clean-Up

At the end of each color run the screen is cleaned thoroughly. It cannot be overemphasized that printing media should not be left to dry in the silk. The screen is laid on newspapers, and all surplus color is scraped out of the screen and off the squeegee with a spatula or a piece of cardboard. If a dye paste has been used, the squeegee and screen are washed under the tap or with a hose and spray attachment. The latter is much more efficient and timesaving. A stiff brush can be used to help clear the silk.

Pigment pastes are washed from the screen with mineral spirits, turpentine, or the remover recommended by the manufacturer. The screen is placed silk side down over newspapers. A small amount of remover is poured directly inside it and washed with rags through the silk onto the newspapers. This is repeated with fresh paper and rags until the stencil and silk are thoroughly clean. Rags soaked with remover will clean the squeegee.

7. Painting and Other Direct Methods

Materials and Equipment

Brushes (nylon)
Paint Rollers
Palette Knife
Spatula (plastic)
Striping Tool

Painting and other direct methods for applying color to fabric are very ancient methods of decoration. Craftsmen have for centuries embellished fabric surfaces in a myriad of designs with simple existing tools. Today we think of this direct approach as one that affords great freedom and spontaneity.

Design Potentials of the Technique

The tools and methods used in direct methods of fabric decoration allow for a great deal of freedom in specific effects and allover design. The obvious result is a design which has no definite repeat of motif, unlike the designs created by printing techniques. In addition, the design is limited in scale only by the size of the fabric being worked on. The approach also offers potential for a variety of con-

Section of a coverlet or hanging, painted and dyed, India, 18th century. (Courtesy of The Cooper Union Museum)

103

tinuous stripe effects which are difficult, if not impossible, with other techniques. The designs to be used require careful planning before execution, since working directly on the fabric does not allow for major changes.

Since the tools used will directly affect the character of the completed design, it is essential to get the feel of the tools as a preliminary procedure. Brushstrokes offer a great variety of design potentials. An enormous range of brushes for painting color on fabric is found in art supply shops and hardware and variety stores. They can be chosen from fine-line widths to as wide as is maneuverable. They come with both long and short, soft and stiff bristles. There are round and flat ones, and tips may be shaped to give sharp edges, or they may be thick and stubby. Experiments with many kinds of brushes will give the designer confidence in his control of the tools. He will recognize how the character of lines and shapes are affected by the tool and how a motif can evolve out of some particular manipulation of that tool. The speed of the stroke, the wetness of the brush, and the position in which it is held are other variables in brushing color on fabric.

Spraying, spattering, and dribbling are other ways to apply dye to fabric, each with a specific effect. Sponges, rollers, cans, and similar devices offer new possibilities for types of lines and textures. The effects created by working on dry and wet surfaces also are among the potentials of this technique. Dye pastes inspire wet-on-wet experiments. They behave much as do watercolors on paper. The fabric can be dampened by spraying with water, or large brushes carrying pale color can saturate the fabric in preparation for the application of darker colors to the damp surface. Wetting the fabric with water will weaken the color subsequently applied, just as adding water or extender to the dye paste does. (If fiber-reactive colors are used, it should be remembered that the water applied to the fabric should contain the chemicals necessary to ensure that the ratio of ingredients in the dye paste is kept constant.)

Preparation

The design can be traced on the fabric over a light box or table. The design may also be transferred with a dressmaker's carbon and tracing wheel, or sketched directly on the fabric with a soft pencil after the fabric is placed on the work table.

The table should be covered with a piece of plastic sheeting to prevent undue saturation of the pad-

Painted tapa cloth, Samoa, 20th century.

Painted cotton, Peru, ca. 1100-1400. (The Textile Museum Washington, D.C.)

104

Details of painted fabrics, showing brushstroke effects.

Painted fabrics, showing wet-on-wet effects.

ding. A clean muslin back cloth is placed over the plastic to absorb the excess dye, and the fabric to be decorated is stretched and pinned over the back cloth.

Procedures

Since the variations possible with direct methods are numerous, it is important to be familiar with the tools used and to achieve the proper dye consistency for them and for the specific fabric to be decorated. The same media are used as in printing techniques, but they must be thinned for ease of application. Each type of fabric behaves in a characteristic way, and to achieve predictable results, some trials should be made. This can be done on one end of the fabric if additional length is allowed. The actual procedure varies according to the effects desired. Some of the possibilities, however, may be mentioned.

In painting, if dry brush effects and sharp edges are desired, it is necessary to let one color dry before applying another that will lie adjacent to or over it. On the other hand, if watered effects and blurred, running edges are desired, the work can progress without pause. If both wet and dry brush effects are desired, the background may be put in first and further detail added after this is dry.

Color may be applied through stencils of plastic, cardboard, or paper, or by brushing, spraying, rolling, or sponging. Plastic spatulas and palette knives, with their resilient blades, can also be used for spreading color or for linear effects.

If a stencil is used, precautions should be taken to keep the color from seeping under the edges. The consistency of the color and careful manipulation of the tool in application will avert such mishaps.

Sprayed color will assume a variety of aspects, depending on the device used and the distance the spray travels to the surface. It can be used to fill clearly defined shapes or can be employed for random effects. The color may be sprayed to achieve solid, graded, or textural effects.

Rollers with various surfaces and in various widths can be purchased from paint supply stores or may be fabricated by the craftsman. The roller must have an absorbent surface to hold the coloring material. The effects produced will vary according to the amount of color carried and the freedom of movement exercised.

Sponges are available in various sizes and shapes. Again, the amount of color carried and the method

Detail of fabric, showing effect of discharge paste applied directly.

"Mountains and Skies," by Berta Wright. A direct method of decoration—"canning" and dye-drawing on silk.

106

of application will affect the visual results considerably.

Sponges and rollers can be used for stripe effects, though the need to replenish the color will not allow for long, unbroken stripes. However, these may be achieved with the "canning" method. A can of any size, with top and bottom smoothly cut away, is placed at the edge of the fabric in an upright position and filled with color of the proper consistency. It then is pulled firmly along the fabric surface from one end of the table to the other. In order to keep the can from being raised as it moves over the ends of the fabric, the fabric can be taped to the table with masking tape. A container can be held under the end of the table to receive the can as it is pulled over the edge. Guides for keeping the lines straight can be made from 2- x 2-inch pine stock of the required length, and attached to the table with clamps. Stripes may be varied freely in direction as well as in width. The width will depend on the sizes of cans the craftsman can collect, or two strips of masking tape can be used to make a stencil over which the can of color is pulled.

A striping tool set available at art supply centers provides a means of creating fine stripes or lines. It consists of a small bottle which holds the medium and also serves as a handle. A replaceable wheel is attached to the bottle, and as it rotates, it carries color to the fabric in very precise lines the width of the wheel. Several wheels of various widths are a part of the set. The choice of size and the maneuverability of the tool inspire diverse effects.

8. Batik and Other Resists

Materials and Equipment

Brushes
Cleaning Fluid
Double Boiler
Flour (wheat and rice)
Heating Unit for Wax
Laundry Starch
Liquid Wax Emulsion
Rubber Gloves
Scraper (plastic)
Stretchers
Tjantings
Waxes (paraffin and beeswax)

Batik is the term used almost universally to describe the process by which a substance is applied to predetermined areas of a fabric for the purpose of resisting subsequent dyeing. The dye-resisting substance most commonly associated with batik is hot wax. Actually, many other materials which will not melt or dissolve when the dye is applied to the fabric can also be used for resists. Other resist materials are basically rosins, fats, and flour pastes.

Design Potentials of the Technique

As with all techniques, the craftsman will better appreciate the scope of the design potentials if he experiments with the materials and tools before proceeding to sketches on paper. He may even devise new tools and materials which serve his purposes better, and experimentation will give him assurance in the control of the implements he chooses to use.

An infinite variety of all the elements of design can be realized with resists. Lines can be made with tjantings, brushes, or syringes. They can be stamped with tools the craftsman designs himself, thus expressing his individuality. The character of shapes will be the result of the choice and manipulation of tools: they can vary in size from the dot made when a wax-loaded brush or tjanting barely touches the fabric to large areas on which the wax is spooned, poured, or brushed with house-painting brushes.

More than one resist used in the same design will give contrasts of edges and surfaces. The craftsman who is familiar with the individual properties of the resists can achieve plain areas as well as crackled

109

A variety of batik effects.

Batik on cotton, Java, 20th century.

Batik on cotton, Java, 19th century. Repeated design made with the tjap stamp. (The Metropolitan Museum of Art, Rogers Fund, 1917)

ones in the same piece. Waxes can be scratched through or scraped; pastes can be combed. Lighted candles can be used to deposit melted wax by dripping. Waxed surfaces can be folded and crackled in specific directions to give emphasis to a design, or they can be crumpled and crushed at random. Various values of one color result from thick and thin applications of the wax because the dye will penetrate faintly in the thinly covered areas, especially with cold wax.

A further possibility with wax resists is to discharge existing color rather than to apply color. Wax is applied to those areas which are to remain the original color of the fabric, and the piece is placed in a discharge bath.

Preparation

Almost any kind of fabric is suitable for decorating by the resist technique if it can be colored with a paste or in a cold dyebath. Very thin fabrics such as silk and cotton organdy, batiste, and chiffon are often used because they accept both resist and dye so readily. However, the uses of these are limited, and very satisfactory results can be realized with linen of all weights, poplin, dress-weight wool, corduroy, velvet, and even terry cloth. The heavier

materials may require application of the resist from both sides if total resistance of the dye is required.

The design may be transferred to the fabric over a light box with soft pencil which will later be washed away. A simple design can be sketched directly on the fabric or transferred with a dressmaker's carbon and tracing wheel.

It is possible to apply a resist without stretching the fabric if something to which the resist will not adhere too stubbornly is placed underneath. In some parts of Asia the fabric is stretched over a table top that is covered with fine sand or china clay. Most craftsmen prefer to have the fabric stretched tautly on a wood frame. Thumbtacks or plastic-topped pushpins are recommended for fastening the fabric to the frame.

Curtain stretchers (such as those used after washing sheer curtains) may be used, and batik supply houses sell special stretchers which are notched so that their size and shape can be changed. Artist's canvas stretchers are useful for small pieces; for yardage, a large frame with cross-piece reinforcements can be made in the length and width the craftsman requires. Pine stock that is 1 x 2 inches can be used. A large stretcher is more convenient if it is either hinged or notched so that it can be dis-

Paste resist decoration on silk, Japan, 20th century.

mantled when not in use. If a large frame is not available, a fabric may be worked on in sections and moved as needed.

HOT WAX RESISTS. The most familiar resist is hot wax, which usually consists of paraffin and beeswax melted together. Paraffin is a mineral-based wax produced by the petroleum industry. A half-and-half mixture is often used, but the proportions may be varied for special effects. The beeswax is soft, and a greater proportion of it will give a flexible surface which will not crackle readily, if at all. A dominance of paraffin will produce a crackle, but it is important to find the proportions which will produce the crackle without peeling. Too much paraffin in the mixture will cause it to crumble and fall away from the surface so that the dye reaches the fabric in areas intended to be undyed, and smudged effects are often the result.

Paraffin and beeswax are easily procurable from grocery and hardware stores. The petroleum industry also produces a variety of other waxes, one of which is similar to beeswax and is much less expensive. (One example is Mobil #2305.) Since it is a bit softer, less is used in the mixture. A proportion of 3 to 1 is a good mixture for experimenting with the materials.

The addition of some kind of fat to the hot wax makes it more adhesive. This is the reason that some craftsmen use melted candle wax, which contains fat, for resists. A fat which can be purchased from drug supply houses for this purpose is stearic acid, a white crystalline substance obtained from tallow and other fats. A good mixture may be made of 5½ parts paraffin, 1 part beeswax, and 3 parts stearic acid.

Javanese batiks are often waxed with a combination of paraffin and rosin. A mixture for experimenting may be made with 1 part paraffin and 3 parts lump rosin. More paraffin will give a more brittle result.

Any shallow utensil, even a coffee can, can be a container for the hot wax. The wax will heat faster if a lid is placed over it. A container equipped with its own electric element is ideal. An electric glue pot makes a good container, but small electric frying pans and roasters, which can sometimes be found in secondhand shops at minimal cost, are even more desirable.

If a heating unit is used, a portable electric stove with a metal plate over the heating element is safer than one in which the wires are exposed. Wax is easily set aflame when it overheats, and the metal plate is good insurance against such accidents. Covers for open heating elements are available in hardware stores.

The temperature of the wax is a matter for experimentation. A temperature of 250°F. is satisfactory, and in a container which has its own temperature regulator, this setting should be used. Every effort should be made to maintain the wax at a constant workable temperature. It is inefficient and frustrating to heat it, remove it from the heat to use, and have to return it in a few moments to heat again.

There will be a trace of smoke from the container when the wax is ready for use. Wax that is too hot will ruin the bristles of a brush instantly. Brushes left standing in the wax against the very hot bottom of the container will be permanently bent or burned away at the tips. Wax which is too hot also tends to spread uncontrollably in the fabric. However, if it is not hot enough, the wax will not penetrate the fibers and will only build up on the surface of the fabric. It may then peel away in the dyebath, allowing the dye to penetrate.

COLD WAX. The liquid wax or wax emulsion used by ceramists for glazing is also of value in fabric decoration. The advantage of this material is that it does not require heating. It is difficult to achieve a strong crackle effect, but if the wax is applied thickly, some veining can be realized. It can be applied with brushes or syringes or by stamping onto the fabric.

PASTE RESISTS. Paste resists have included such ingredients as rice, bran, and wheat flours, salt, laundry starch, kaolin, and various gums. A very simple flour resist can be made with 3 tablespoons flour mixed with 1 cup cold water. The paste is placed in the top of a double boiler and cooked until it becomes semitransparent. It should be stirred constantly. While hot, it is brushed or spooned thickly over the fabric.

Another resist paste can be made with 1 ounce white flour, 1 ounce rice flour, ½ ounce laundry starch, and 1¼ cups hot water. The dry ingredients are mixed with a small amount of cold water until the lumps have been worked out. The hot water is added, and the mixture is cooked in the top of a double boiler for about 15 minutes. The paste

A variety of batik effects achieved with hot wax.

should be kept warm while it is being applied to the fabric.

Procedures

The fabric to be decorated is laid over wax paper or aluminum foil on the work table, or fastened to a stretcher which is laid on a table or propped on two objects such as sawhorses to hold it at a convenient height. If hot wax is to be used, the heating unit and container are placed safely and conveniently in relation to the work.

The procedure consists of applying resist to those areas which are to remain the color of the fabric, dyeing the fabric, and drying it. More resist is applied to retain some of the second color, and the fabric is dyed, dried, and waxed again, etc. (Dyes which contain alkalies, such as the fiber-reactives, cause the wax to begin to disintegrate after only two applications and two immersions in the dyebath. All waxed areas may have to be rewaxed, or it may be expedient to remove all the wax, put the piece through a detergent bath, and begin waxing again.)

The resist is applied to the cloth with whatever tools seem most appropriate for the specific design and fabric being used. Brushes of all sizes, shapes, and types of bristle are useful for all resists. A special tool used for applying hot wax to the fabric is the tjanting. It is a small metal cup with one or more spouts and fitted with a wood or bamboo handle. It is dipped in the container of wax to fill the cup and, with a bit of cloth held under it to prevent dripping, the wax is deposited on the cloth in dots or lines. The craftsman should experiment to find the most convenient way to hold the tool, as well as at what temperature the wax flows from it most satisfactorily. A syringe or a cake-decorating tube can be used as well as a brush for cold resists, and both hot and cold resists can be stamped on the fabric.

All resists are left to dry thoroughly before dyeing is begun. Fabrics treated with resists which contain rosin are usually left for several days before dyeing. To apply the color, the piece can be immersed in a dyebath after each waxing, or it can be left on the stretcher and the dye brushed or sponged on selected areas or the whole, depending on the nature of the design. If it is likely that the resist will not withstand the crushing and rubbing apt to occur in a bath of color, it is wiser to leave the piece on the stretcher to apply the color. In brushing on the color, less dye enters from underneath, where the resist may not have penetrated. However, the varia-

Use of the tjanting to apply hot wax.

Batik done with tjanting and brush.

Batik done with a brush.

Resist decoration, printed and drawn.

tion of color resulting from thick and thin applications of resist may be desired, and in this event the uneven penetration is encouraged. When the dye is applied with a brush, it is more manageable if it contains a small amount of thickening.

When a crackle effect is desirable, more crisp, clean lines result if the waxed fabric is chilled before crackling. This may be accomplished by placing it in the refrigerator, dampening it under cold water, or leaving it out of doors during cold weather. The crackling can also be the result of crowding the waxed cloth into a dyebath. If the dye is to be brushed on, any crackle desired can be accomplished by pushing against the waxed surfaces from underneath or by removing the fabric from the frame, crushing it between the hands, and tacking it down again to receive the dye. More controlled crackling results from folding vertically, diagonally, or horizontally. Many craftsmen leave the crackle process until the last, and usually the darkest, color is applied. With this method dark veins of color spread throughout the piece and often contribute a harmonizing effect. However, it is possible to plan to reserve the lines in various colors by waxing over them after each crackling and dyeing.

In applying dye with a brush or sponge, it will be noted that excess liquid collects on the surface of the wax. If left undisturbed, these drops of color can be used to achieve another kind of textural effect. When a hot iron is used to remove the wax, the color is pushed down into the fabric and clings there. However, if this effect is not desired, the drops of color can be removed from a heavy deposit of wax. Paper is placed over the wax and ironed with a slightly warm iron. The drops will adhere to the paper. They can also be wiped away from the wax with a damp sponge or cloth, or the surface can be scraped with a blunt tool such as a plastic scraper.

Resist materials should be thoroughly removed from the fabric. A surface which retains wax will soil easily, and the dark rings left in and around wax-impregnated areas seldom enhance the design. The method of removal depends on the type of dye used as well as on the resist. The starch pastes may be removed by soaking the fabric in cool water and washing it in warm detergent baths, scratching and gently rubbing away the paste.

The most usual method of removing wax is to place the fabric between several layers of newspaper and iron it until no more wax will come away on the paper. Wax emulsion resist is also ironed out be-

tween layers of paper; it is easier to remove than the hot wax. If the dyes permit, it may also be removed by boiling in a detergent bath, by repeated washings in warm water, or with cleaning fluid. Several methods are used for removing heavy deposits of hot wax. If it is important to save the wax for future use, the fabric can be laid flat and the wax scraped away with a dull plastic scraper (such as that used to remove ice from a car windshield). Slightly heating the surface will hasten the process. The wax will crumple and shred away from the surface if rubbed between the hands. Rubber gloves are recommended to protect the hands from the abrasion caused by this process.

The above methods are only the first steps in removing the wax, since there will always be some wax left in the fabric. The last vestiges are removed either by washing the fabric in a hot detergent bath and rinsing it in cold water several times, or by working it in a bath of cleaning fluid. Several other fluids that will remove the wax are kerosene, carbon tetrachloride, xylol, and benzene. However, some of these are fire hazards, others have toxic fumes. A commercial cleaning fluid serves the purpose and is much safer for studio work. It should be noted that if the wax has been removed in order to apply more dye, the fabric must be soaped and rinsed to remove the cleaning fluid before redyeing.

Batik crackle.

Paste resist crackle.

Discharge batik crackle.

9. Tie-Dye

Materials and Equipment

Button and Carpet Thread
Cotton Cord (12-ply)
Raffia
Rubber Gloves
Sewing Needles
Sheet Plastic
Straight Pins
Wood Scraps

Tie-dye is a resist technique in which the pattern is achieved by dyeing it into the fabric rather than by applying it to the surface. The pattern is the result of reserving some areas by tieing, knotting, folding, or sewing them so that dye cannot penetrate. Other areas are either left free or loosely held so that they are colored.

Design Potentials of the Technique

Before making definite design plans for tie-dyeing, the craftsman should gather, fold, pleat, twist, and otherwise manipulate a piece of fabric in order to better visualize the design possibilities as well as the limitations of the technique. The effects of tieing the fabric in a variety of ways can be studied in small experiments. The size of the wrapping material together with the tightness of wrapping will affect the results. Several methods for achieving pattern can be combined in one piece. Cords for wrapping can be dyed beforehand and not rinsed so that color will bleed into the fabric. Textured effects can serve as backgrounds for definite shapes. Shapes can vary in size and character and can be arranged in bands, borders, or allover patterns.

There are enough accidental effects even with the most well planned and executed designs to make tie-dyeing an intriguing craft. It is necessary to plan the tieing and adhere to the measurements marked if a well organized design is to result.

Preparation

The fabric is ironed and spread on a table so the pattern to be followed can be marked on it. A soft pencil is used to mark lightly the widths of folds and indicate the areas to be tied or lines to be stitched. In some instances, as for the center of a circle, a dot will serve. A piece of thin cardboard is convenient for measuring and marking repeated shapes or sizes. A metal measuring tape, yardstick, or ruler may be used for accurate division of areas. Pins will hold arrangements of the fabric until they can be tied.

The craftsman will find that the position of the pattern in relation to the straight of the weave must be controlled for satisfactory design results. It is necessary to check the edges of the fabric to see that there is no slipping or pulling which will distort the pattern.

Procedures

TIEING. A 12-ply cotton cord, available at paper supply houses, is recommended for most tie-dye projects. It is strong enough to bind securely even the heaviest fabrics, and the large size of the cord is timesaving when wrapping large areas. Raffia is another strong material which is useful for tieing especially heavy fabrics.

Sheet plastic of a medium weight which can be purchased by the yard is used for tieing off wide areas that are not to be colored or to protect already dyed parts. (A thin plastic is easily pierced when manipulating the tied fabric in the dyebath, and a very heavy one resists secure tieing.) The plastic is wrapped around the pleated, folded, or gathered fabric several times and tied firmly with the cord. Immersion in a boiling dyebath does not harm it.

To start tieing off an area, the gathered fabric is held in the left hand, and the cord is twisted around it at least twice at the edge of the area to be tied off.

Fabric tied to create circular shapes.

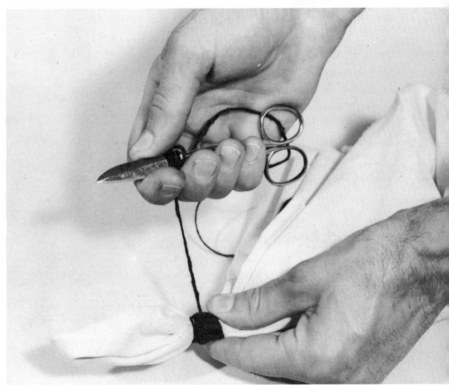

Scissors are used as a bar to pull binding tight.

The short end of the cord is held under the thumb, 3 or 4 inches from the end. The long end of the cord is pulled tight with the right hand, and a knot is tied. The cord is then wrapped and pulled until the area is covered sufficiently, and then wound back to the beginning for the final knotting. If the dye is to be completely resisted, the area should be closely covered with wrapping, each twist of cord lying against or slightly over the last. Several layers will provide further resistance. The binding can be pulled more tightly and the fingers saved from painful cuts if the cord is wound around a pair of scissors to create a bar for pulling.

If it is planned that the dye should enter between the bindings to create a repeated pattern, both the direction of the wrappings and the distance between them must be controlled. Wide or narrow bands at right angles to the length of the piece result from wrapping solidly straight across the gathered fabric, knotting, and cutting the cord, and repeating this procedure at planned intervals. Angular lines develop if the cord is carried along from one end to the other of a wide area with space left between each wrapping. If then, in returning to the beginning knot, the wrapping crosses the first binding, a crisscross pattern results.

Sharp, definite edges occur when the binding is pulled very tight. Patterned edges result when the cord is knotted around the fabric a bit loosely at first and gradually tightened as the wrapping progresses. The dye will run down the creases of the loosely bound parts, and small repeated shapes will result, while the tightly held areas will resist the dye altogether. If there is doubt that the cord will keep the dye out of the fabric, some form of wax or paste resist can be brushed over the binding and over as much surrounding area as desired. (This method cannot be used with hot dyeing.)

Untieing is always left until the piece is at least semidry. Wet dye will migrate into the resist areas and destroy the sharpness of pattern if the fabric is untied. After dyeing and drying, the knots are cut and the cord is unwound. To avoid the possibility of cutting holes in the fabric, the cord is cut against the knot at the beginning or end of the tieing. The leftover end of the cord is pulled until there is enough space to slip the blade of the scissors inside. The cord is cut and unwound to the next knot, which is pulled away from the fabric and cut.

A variety of allover effects possible with tie-dye.

Fold-and-dye with fiber-reactive dyes, by Ronald Goodman.

Tie-dye on linen, by Meda Parker Johnston.

Fabric pleated and tied.

Patterns created by pleating, tieing, and dyeing.

PLEATING. Pleating and tieing a length of fabric is one of the most logical ways to achieve a repeated pattern. A piece of paper can be folded to find what possibilities are presented by this approach as well as what problems will arise. Two methods of pleating should be considered. Beginning at one side or end, the piece is accordion-pleated to the other side or end. In this way the outer edges remain outside. If the piece is folded in the center and the sides or ends are brought to the middle repeatedly until the pleats are as narrow as desired, it will be found that the central part of the piece will have been brought to the outside. This is of concern because the areas brought to the outside will receive the heaviest concentration of dye.

If the fabric is pleated vertically, the designs will be horizontal; horizontal pleats will produce vertical designs. Diagonal pleating results in diagonal design, but if the fabric is folded in the center and then the double cloth is pleated diagonally, a zigzag pattern will develop.

The piece of fabric is spread on a table and measured so that the pleats will divide it evenly. The width of the pleats is marked with a pencil, and the fabric is folded on the marks. Straight pins are used to hold the fabric in place until it is steam-ironed.

The pleated strip can be wrapped at intervals to create bands or stripes. The unbound areas will receive the first dyeing. When the fabric is semidry, some of the first color can be covered with wrapping to reserve it, while some of the first bindings can be untied so that these areas can receive a second color. Some of the colored areas can be left open to be overdyed by the second color. With two dyeings, therefore, there will be bands of the two colors as well as some bands with a third color created by overdyeing. The original color of the cloth under any of the first wrapping may give a fourth color. Further color effects can be achieved by brushing contrasting or darker-colored dye on outer edges. The location of these areas in the opened piece must be visualized so that scattered, unrelated effects are avoided.

The pleated strip can be folded at right angles to the pleats and tied to hold the folds in place as well as to create a variety of shapes. Other kinds of shapes can be made with the pleated strip by wrapping it around an object such as a piece of wood and tying it securely. The edges pressed against the object will not receive the dye, while the outer surfaces will receive as much or as little as the binding allows. Twisting the piece as it is wrapped around the object will expose parts of both sides of the strip to the dye.

TWISTING. Twisting and dyeing a length of fabric will give random textural effects. Experiments will show that various fabrics accept or reject the dye in different ways according to the special characteristics of weave, weight, and fiber.

The fabric is spread on a table and either gathered or pleated into a narrow strip. This can be done horizontally, vertically, or diagonally. The ends are tied very securely, and one end is fastened to an immovable object, such as a doorknob. While the total length is kept taut, the piece is twisted until it coils. The ends of the coil are placed together and wrapped with cord to hold the twist securely. This tight bundle will reject most of the dye except on the exposed areas. Larger pattern and deeper penetration of the dye may be expected if the least possible wrapping is used. Less pattern and less penetration will result from close wrapping, a broken pattern from rather open wrapping. It should be remembered that the direction of the wrapping will affect the design.

The bundle is immersed in a dyebath until the desired color and penetration are achieved. It is removed and allowed to become semidry before unwrapping and untwisting. The pattern probably will be scattered, and more twisting, wrapping, and dyeing may be done to bring undyed areas to the surface and to overdye some of the first color. The process is repeated as many times as necessary to attain an even distribution of color and pattern. Other colors can be introduced by brushing the dye over selected areas or by wrapping the bundle with predyed cord.

Steps in twisting a pleated fabric.

Pattern created by twisting, tieing, and dyeing.

FOLDING.   Folding and dyeing without tieing can result in a controlled allover pattern of contrasting lines, shapes, and colors. A thin fabric which will allow the dye to penetrate quickly is recommended.

Very accurate measurements are required to achieve repeated pattern. The fabric is folded horizontally, vertically, or diagonally to create a strip. Further folding at right angles to the lengthwise folds will make a stack of rectangles or squares. Triangles will be formed if these shapes are folded diagonally. All edges should be ironed as the work progresses, preferably with a steam iron.

Steps in dip-dyeing a folded fabric.

Patterns resulting from folding and dyeing.

The firmly held folded fabric is lowered into a dyebath to the depth that will produce the planned shapes. Dipping different edges may create stripes or plaids. An intricate pattern will result if each corner and edge is dipped in a separate dyebath. The piece can be tilted while held in the dye to produce still other shapes. When the desired depth of color is achieved, the fabric is removed and squeezed carefully and thoroughly to extract all excess dye. If several colors are to be used, the excess dye is removed after each dipping. It is not necessary to dry the fabric between dyebaths. When the dyeing is completed, the dyed piece is immediately unfolded and spread flat to dry. Some touching-up can be done with a brush dipped in dye.

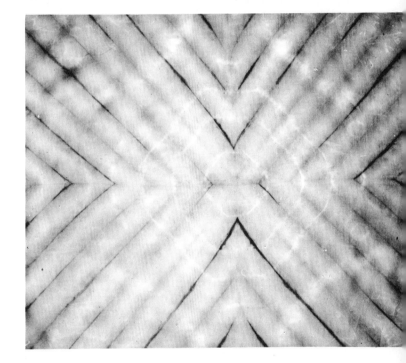

KNOTTING. Knotting a pleated or gathered length of fabric will result in large, bold shapes. Thin fabric is more successful than others for this method of achieving pattern.

If a repetition of the motif is planned, an experimental knot will show the amount of fabric needed for one knot. The fabric is marked on each side of the knot, and when it is untied, a measurement of the space used is taken. A plan which allows for the amount needed for each knot and the space to be left between the knots is made. To achieve a pattern which will lie straight on the fabric, it is important to tie the center knot and then work toward the ends on each side, adjusting the fabric to keep the edges even at all times. Care must be taken to tie each knot in the same manner and then to adjust them by tightening or loosening, so that there will be similarity of shape and size. If the knots are arranged some distance apart, they can be dyed separately in several colors. It is also possible to hold the knots together above the dyebath and immerse only the spaces between the knots. After dyeing, the piece is allowed to become at least semidry before untieing if definite edges are desired. After untieing, more knots between or overlapping the first ones can provide further pattern and color variations.

TIEING SHAPES. It is possible to pull up tufts of fabric and tie them into individual motifs in a variety of shapes. Traditionally the shapes have been circles, diamonds, or squares. They can vary in size from areas so small that a needle is needed to hold the fabric while tieing to those as large as the width of the fabric allows.

To some extent the weight of the fabric will govern the size of the shapes: very small shapes require a finely woven fabric. However, even velveteen and corduroy can be tied for shapes on a larger scale.

The cloth is spread on a table and the plan for the placement of the shapes is indicated with penciled dots. The shapes can be arranged in an allover design that covers large areas, in stripes or borders, or they can be contained within other shapes. The dots indicate the centers of the shapes. For small ones a needle is used to pick up the dot and hold the center so that the fabric can be smoothed downward and tied as near or as far from the center as desired. The manner in which the fabric is pulled from the center point will influence the resulting shape. The larger the shape, the more care is required in distributing the fabric into even folds or gathers so that it can be tied into place. The distance from the center dot to the tie will be the radius of the circle or half the width of the diamond or square. Rings will result from bands of wrapping, while the tuft can be wrapped partially to create a patterned shape, or totally to create a solid shape. Tufts can be dyed separately in a variety of colors and then wrapped to resist a background color.

To make large, complex symmetrical shapes, the fabric is folded and pinned in place. Half the shape is drawn against the fold. A cardboard pattern may be used to outline the shape if an exact repeat is desired. The doubled cloth is pleated evenly following the outline and then wrapped carefully. The wrapping should be exactly on top of the penciled line.

Pebbles, seeds, plastic or glass objects, pieces of wood, cork, etc., can be tied inside a tuft of fabric to create a variety of shapes. An experiment will indicate the amount of fabric required for one motif, and allowance for this amount should be made in planning the placement of motifs over a large area.

Shapes created by planned tieing and dyeing.

Silk sari with pattern resulting from stitching and dyeing, India, 19th century. (Courtesy of The Brooklyn Museum)

Cotton carrying cloth, stitched and dyed with indigo, Nigeria, 20th century. (Courtesy of The Cooper Union Museum)

STITCHING. Stitching is another method for creating areas which will resist dye. All kinds of motifs can be executed with either a running or a whipping stitch. Shapes can be abstract, such as stripes, diamonds, ovals, or circles, or they can represent natural forms. Intricate details can be produced as long as the shape can be outlined with stitches and pulled up tightly. The knot left at the beginning of the stitching is made large and strong enough to withstand the pulling necessary for satisfactory resistance to the dye.

Shapes are drawn or traced lightly in pencil on the fabric. If the shape is symmetrical, half of it can be traced against the fold of a doubled cloth. The piece is pinned securely, and running stitches are made through the two layers. Several rows of stitching inside the shape will give bolder effects and more complex patterns. The needle and thread from each row of stitching are left hanging until all are completed, since it is very difficult to sew on fabric which has some parts already gathered. The finished sewing is pulled up and held firmly while being fastened off. The stitches can be fastened off by tieing the ends together or by backstitching. A single layer of fabric can be stitched, but it is more difficult to achieve a shape with definite edges in this way. Several rows of running stitches inside the shape will reinforce the outline.

The whipping stitch is more effective than the running stitch on a single layer of fabric. Very complex shapes can be drawn with pencil and a row of whipping placed over the outline with either small or long stitches. This will create patterned outlines. As the work progresses, the stitches are pulled firmly, but the gathering is left until all stitching is completed. In gathering whipped stitches, the head of the needle can be slipped under a stitch here and there to move along the excess thread and help pull it more tightly. The whipping stitch is usually fastened off by backstitching several times.

Stitches can vary in direction. The same line can be whipped from left to right and the stitches returning from the right made to cross those of the first row. More variety can be introduced by using running stitches in several rows and then whipping over them.

When several rows of stitches are placed close together, some can be pulled up to resist the first dyeing, and others tightened to resist the second. The first ones tightened can then be released to receive the second color, etc.

DYEING. The most desirable dye will be one which gives the strongest color in the shortest time. Most pieces will be tied in such a manner that the bulk is reduced and only small baths are necessary. These can be given in bowls for cold baths or shallow pans for hot ones.

Because dyestuffs color at different rates of time, an interesting phenomenon occurs when two colors are mixed in the dyebath to achieve a third. For example, orange and turquoise blue may be mixed to obtain an olive green. After dyeing the tied piece, it will be found that the colors separate around the ties. The one that colors the fabric faster forms a halo on the edges of the green areas.

Sharper, clearer resists usually result from dampening the tied piece before entering it in the dyebath.

Running stitch, flat and drawn up.

Whipping stitch, flat and drawn up.

The usual procedure is to begin with light colors and progress to dark ones in the dyeing. However, this is not an absolute rule, since it may be desirable to dye a light color after dark ones in order to color areas which were tied during previous baths.

Experiments with small tied pieces will help determine how strong the bath should be and how long the fabric should remain in it. The dyed piece may be left unrinsed until it has dried to allow the dye to penetrate the fibers more thoroughly.

A further possibility for obtaining design through tieing is to discharge existing color rather than to apply color. The tied fabric is placed in the discharge solution. Varying degrees of color value are possible when the action is watched closely, and the fabric is removed and rinsed when the desired result is seen. The piece can be tied further to retain some of the darker values and dipped in the solution again to obtain lighter ones. When as much color has been discharged as desired, the piece should be rinsed and untied immediately. The fabric should then be washed to completely remove the bleach.

Effects achieved by tieing and discharging.

10. Dyes and Pigments

A dye properly chosen and applied will penetrate the fiber and become a part of the fabric. The cloth will retain its natural luster and softness of hand. No one dye will successfully dye all types of fibers or react in the same way to all aftertreatments. The dyer often must sacrifice one attribute for another: brilliance of color may have to be given up to ensure washfastness, or washfastness given up to attain brilliance of color.

Universal fastness tests are used by dye manufacturers for evaluating their colors, and these findings are shown in their catalogues. The craftsman will choose the colors which are most suitable for the conditions and requirements of his own work. It is not necessary to use colors of only one brand. The hue the craftsman prefers may be more washfast in one brand than in another. The method of application will be the same within each class of dyestuff. The differences in formulas given by various manufacturers are usually in the assistants called for. (Often the assistant is sold under a name given by the dye manufacturer.) A list of Chemicals and Assistants is provided on page 149.

Fiber Identification

The selection of a dyestuff depends on the fiber content of the fabric to be decorated. If the craftsman does not know the fiber content of a fabric, a simple burning test may be used to identify at least the family group to which it belongs. (It should be noted that cellulosic fibers which have been mercerized are more desirable for dyeing purposes than untreated ones. The chemicals used in the mercerizing process improve the affinity between the fiber and the dye.)

A few threads are unraveled from both warp and weft of the fabric to be identified. They are tested separately by holding with tweezers over a flame long enough to note their reaction.

NATURAL FIBERS. *Cellulosic fibers* (cotton, linen, and viscose rayon) burn readily and continue burning even after the flame is removed. An odor of burning paper is given off.

Protein fibers (silk and wool) burn only while held in the flame. A soft black ash is formed, and an odor of burning hair or feathers is given off.

SYNTHETIC FIBERS. *Acetate* and *acrylics* melt and shrink away from the flame, forming a hard black bead. An odor of acetic acid is typical.

Nylon melts away from the flame, forming a hard, tan-colored bead. A chemical odor is given off.

Polyester (Dacron) burns slowly and melts. A hard black or brown bead is formed. A chemical odor is given off.

The selection of a dyestuff (or pigment) also depends on the attributes of the various media and the technique to be used in decorating the fabric. The following tables may be of use to the craftsman in making his choice:

ATTRIBUTES OF MEDIA

Medium	Brilliance of Color	Washfastness (in lukewarm water)	Boilfastness	Lightfastness (to natural light)
Acid dyes	X	X		X
Basic dyes	X	X		
Direct dyes		X		X
Disperse dyes	X	X		X
Fiber-reactive dyes	X	X	X	X
Household dyes		X		X
Prepared vat dyes		X	X	X
Soluble vat dyes	X	X	X	X
Mineral colors		X	X	X
Pigments	X	X		X

MEDIA, FABRICS, AND METHODS OF APPLICATION

Medium	Hot Baths	Cold Baths	Printing Pastes
Acid dyes	S W Syn		S W Syn
Basic dyes	C* L* V* S W	C* L* V* S W	C L V S W
Direct dyes	C L V S W		C K V S W
Disperse dyes	S W Syn		S W Syn
Fiber-reactive dyes		C L V	C L V S
Household dyes	C L V S W Syn		C L V S W Syn
Prepared vat dyes			C L V S
Soluble vat dyes		C L V	C L V
Mineral colors		C L V	
Pigments			C L V S W Syn

C   Cotton   *Fabric must be premordanted.
L   Linen
S   Silk
Syn Synthetics (nylon, polyester, rayon acetate)
V   Viscose rayon
W   Wool

Color Value and Concentration of Dye or Pigment

Color value in hot and cold dyeing is determined by the amount of dyestuff used in the dyebath in relation to the weight of the fabric being dyed. Color value in dye and pigment pastes is determined by the ratio of dye or pigment to the other components of the formula. The beginner will have no way of knowing how much dye or pigment to use to obtain a certain color value. This knowledge is built up through experience, and a record in the form of a notebook containing color swatches and notes on how each was obtained is invaluable. Among dyers this is known as a pattern book.

The strength of a color is defined in terms of percentage. The following table will provide a rough guide for achieving the desired color value (except when otherwise specified in the formula):

Color Value	% of Dyestuff (in relation to weight of fabric)
Deep	3 to 5%
Medium	1 to 3%
Pale	½ to 1%

The formulas are worked out in advance, with X% representing the depth of value desired. The amounts of all other components are also expressed as percentages of the weight of the fabric. The amount of water is expressed as a ratio of the weight of the liquor to the weight of the fabric.

It is preferable to use the metric system in work with dyestuffs because the small amounts that are used may be more accurately measured on a gram scale. To convert pounds and ounces to grams, the following equivalents may be used:

$$1 \text{ ounce} = 28.35 \text{ grams}$$
$$1 \text{ pound} = 453.60 \text{ grams}$$

The formulas are worked out as in the following sample: 500 grams of fabric is to be dyed a 5% shade. The formula is:

X% dyestuff
4% acetic acid
20% salt
10 to 1 liquor ratio

To find the weight of dyestuff needed for the 5% shade, 5% of the weight of the fabric is computed:

500 (grams of fabric) x .05 = 25 (grams of dyestuff)

To find the weight of acetic acid needed, 4% of the weight of the fabric is computed:

50 (grams of fabric) x .04 = 20 (grams of acid)

To find the weight of salt needed, 20% of the weight of the fabric is computed:

500 (grams of fabric) x .20 = 100 (grams of salt)

To find the weight of water needed, the weight of the fabric is multiplied by 10:

500 (grams of fabric) x 10 = 5,000 (grams of water)

In pastes, the amount of dyestuff and other components is expressed as parts by weight in relation to 1,000 parts of paste. It is recommended that the parts be translated into grams, since 1,000 grams is a convenient amount of dye paste (approximately 4½ cups) to work with. If a smaller quantity is needed, the formula can be reduced by a half, a quarter, etc.

The following table will provide a rough guide for achieving the desired color value:

Color Value	Parts of Dyestuff (per 1,000 parts of paste)
Deep	50 to 70
Medium	30 to 50
Pale	5 to 30

The color value achieved with pigments depends on the amount of extender added to the pigment. No general guides can be given for the proportions to be used because pigments vary greatly. Most manufacturers will suggest the amount of extender to be added; the craftsman should experiment for the best results.

Dyebaths

Distilled water is ideal for dyeing. However, this is expensive, and the dyer can use water softened by a device that is permanently installed or can add Calgon (sodium hexametaphosphate) to the water. A teaspoon of Calgon for each quart of water is recommended.

Since the amounts of water used in dyebaths are large, it is convenient to convert the gram weight calculated in the formula into a fluid measure such as cups, quarts, or gallons. The following equivalents may be used:

Weight	Volume
33 grams	1 fluid ounce
272 grams	1 cup
1,094 grams	1 quart
4,376 grams	1 gallon

Thus, the 5,000 grams of water needed for the sample formula above would be converted into 1 gallon + 18 fluid ounces.

It should be noted that the amount of water in the dyebath has nothing to do with the depth of color produced on the fabric being dyed. Less water in the bath may cause the dye to be taken up more quickly, but the color will be no darker, and the fabric may be spotted from being too crowded in the shorter bath. Similarly, more water than recommended will not lighten the color. It will only slow down the dyeing process, because it will take longer to reach the temperature at which the dye uptake is energetic.

It is possible to adjust the dyebath to achieve a darker value by adding extra dye in the form of a solution. The fabric must be removed from the bath before the color is added. In hot dyeing the bath must be cooled to about 160°F. before adding the color.

A container large enough to allow free movement of the fabric is necessary for level dyeing, or even coloring. In hot and cold dyeing a stainless steel or enamel container can be used; plastic containers can be used for cold dyeing. Stainless steel "stock pots" are available from restaurant supply houses, and enamel preserving kettles or baby tubs may be found in hardware stores.

For hot dyeing the liquor ratio recommended is usually 30 to 1. This gives ample space for the movement of dye through the fabric, an important factor in level dyeing. A shorter liquor ratio is used in cold dyeing, sometimes as little as 5 to 1.

Two rules must always be observed in all dyeing: (1) The fabric must be removed from the dyebath before anything is added. (2) After anything is added, the dyebath must be thoroughly stirred before the fabric is re-entered.

Hot Dyeing

Dyeing in hot baths is usual when an allover color is required to begin with and for discharge techniques. Many craftsmen also prefer hot baths for tie-dyeing.

After the fabric is pretreated (see Chapter 4), it must be wet-out, or dampened, before it is entered in a hot bath. Most fibers will be damaged if they are exposed to extreme changes of temperature. The fabric should not be plunged into a boiling bath from a cold one, or removed from a boiling bath to a cold rinse. It is entered at about 120°F., and then the temperature of the bath is raised gradually. The uptake of the dye in the hot bath is rapid within the first 15 minutes after the temperature specified in the directions is reached. Thereafter it is gradual, until the fabric will not accept any more. The fabric should be kept under the surface of the dyebath and moved about from time to time to avoid spotting. When the dyeing is finished, the fabric is rinsed several times in baths of progressively cooler water.

ACID DYES

Silk

    X% dyestuff

   10% common salt

    2% glacial acetic acid

 1 to 3% sulfuric acid (diluted by adding to 1 cup cold water)

    5% synthetic detergent

 30 to 1 liquor ratio

Method:

The dyestuff is pasted in a small amount of cold water, and enough hot water to dissolve it is added. This solution, the salt, and the detergent are stirred into the warm bath. The fabric is entered, and the temperature is raised slowly to 160°F. At this point the fabric is removed, the acetic acid is stirred in, and the fabric is re-entered. The temperature is raised slowly to 190°F. The fabric is removed, the sulfuric acid stirred in, and the fabric re-entered. (Sulfuric acid should be poured down the side of the container to avoid spattering.) The dyeing is continued at 190°F. for 45 minutes.

Wool

(Some acid dyes use acetic acid, others sulfuric acid, as the exhausting agent with wool. The acid needed for the particular dyestuff is not always specified by the manufacturer, and the craftsman must experiment to determine which one is needed.)

Formula #1

    X% dyestuff

 10 to 15% common salt (light to dark values)

  3 to   5% sulfuric acid (diluted by adding to 1 cup cold water)

   30 to 1 liquor ratio

Formula #2

    X% dyestuff

 10 to 15% common salt (light to dark values)

  1 to   2% glacial acetic acid

   30 to 1 liquor ratio

Method:

The same as for silk, except that in Formula #2 the fabric is removed after simmering for 30 minutes at 190°F., and ½ to 1% more acetic acid is stirred in.

Acrylics

    X% dyestuff

    2% sulfuric acid

  30 to 1 liquor ratio

Method:

The same as for silk and wool, except that the acid is stirred in at 200°F., and the dyeing is continued at this temperature for 1 hour.

Nylon

    X% dyestuff

    4% ammonium acetate

  30 to 1 liquor ratio

Method:

The dyestuff is pasted in a small amount of cold water, and enough hot water to dissolve it is added.

This solution and the ammonium acetate are stirred into the warm bath. The fabric is entered, and the temperature is raised slowly to 205°F. The dyeing is continued at this temperature for 30 minutes. If exhaustion is poor, ½% acetic acid may be stirred in.

BASIC DYES

Cotton, linen, and viscose rayon will not accept basic dyes unless premordanted. There are two methods for mordanting: the dyebath for basic dyes is the same for fabric mordanted by either method.

Tannic acid and tartar emetic mordant

The amounts of the chemicals used are based on the amount of dyestuff used. The stronger the color value, the stronger the mordant bath must be. The following table will serve as a guide:

% of Dyestuff	% of Tannic Acid
0.10%	0.5%
0.25%	1.0%
0.50%	1.5%
1.00%	3.0%
2.00%	8.0%

The amount of tartar emetic is half that of the tannic acid.

Method:

The tannic acid powder is dissolved in a small amount of boiling water. The solution is added to the bath. The fabric is entered, and the temperature is raised to 110°F. and maintained there for 3 hours. The fabric should be kept completely submerged with weights. The fabric is left overnight in the cooling bath.

The tartar emetic is dissolved in a small amount of boiling water, and the solution is added to a fresh bath. The fabric is removed from the tannic acid bath, wrung out, and placed in the tartar emetic bath for about 30 minutes. It is then removed, wrung out, and entered immediately in the dyebath.

For increased fastness, the fabric can be back-tanned (mordanted again after dyeing) in the same tannic acid and tartar emetic baths. While still wet from the dyebath, the well-rinsed fabric is entered in the tannic acid bath for 30 minutes, wrung out, and entered in the tartar emetic bath for 15 minutes. It is then rinsed again and dried.

Direct dye mordant

Direct dyes can be used as a mordant for fabric to be dyed with basic dyes.

> X% dyestuff
> 5 to 50% common salt (light to dark values)
> 30 to 1 liquor ratio

Method:

The dyestuff is pasted with the cold water, and enough hot water to dissolve it is added. This solution is stirred into the warm bath, and the fabric is entered. The temperature is raised slowly to 180°F., and the dyeing is continued at this temperature for 45 minutes. The dyed fabric is rinsed and transferred to the bath of basic dye. If the fabric is dried, it must be wet-out before dyeing with the basic dye.

Cotton, linen, and viscose rayon
> X% dyestuff
> ½ to 1% glacial acetic acid
> 30 to 1 liquor ratio

Method:

The dyestuff is pasted with the acetic acid, and enough hot water to dissolve it is added. This solution is stirred into the warm bath. The fabric is entered, and the temperature is raised slowly to 180°F. The dyeing is continued at this temperature for 30 minutes.

Silk
> X% dyestuff
> ½ to 1% synthetic detergent
> ½% glacial acetic acid
> 30 to 1 liquor ratio

Method:

The same as for cotton, linen, and viscose rayon, except that the detergent is stirred into the bath with the solution, and the dyeing is continued for 15 minutes.

Wool
> X% dyestuff
> ½ to 1% glacial acetic acid
> 30 to 1 liquor ratio

Method:

The same as for cotton, linen, and viscose rayon, except that the dyeing is continued for 15 minutes.

DIRECT DYES

Cotton and linen
> X% dyestuff
> 5 to 50% common salt (light to dark values)
> 30 to 1 liquor ratio

Method:

The dyestuff is pasted with a small amount of cold water, and enough hot water to dissolve it is added. This solution is stirred into the warm bath. The fabric is entered, and the temperature is raised slowly. A quarter of the salt is stirred into the bath at 10-minute intervals; the fabric is removed and re-entered for each addition. The temperature is raised to 200°F., and the dyeing is continued at this temperature for 45 minutes.

Viscose rayon
Method:

The same as for cotton and linen, except that the temperature is raised to 180°F., and half the salt is stirred in at 10-minute intervals. The fabric is removed and re-entered for each addition. The dyeing is continued for 10 minutes after the second addition of salt.

Silk
Method:

The same as for cotton and linen, except that the temperature should only be raised to 190°F. (higher temperatures reduce the luster of silk). If necessary, ½ to 1% glacial acetic acid may be added to help exhaust the dyebath.

Wool
Method:

The same as for cotton and linen, except that the temperature is raised to 190°F., and the dyeing is continued at this temperature for 30 minutes. If necessary, ½ to 1% glacial acetic acid may be added to help exhaust the dyebath.

DISPERSE DYES

Silk, wool, and synthetics
    X% dyestuff
      1% synthetic detergent
    30 to 1 liquor ratio
Method:

The dyestuff is pasted with the detergent, and enough hot water to dissolve it is added. This solution is stirred into the warm bath. The fabric is entered, and the temperature is raised slowly to 175°F. The dyeing is continued at this temperature for 30 minutes.

HOUSEHOLD DYES

Directions for use are supplied by the manufacturer.

Cold Dyeing

Some fabric decoration techniques require cold baths. They are necessary for resist techniques when paste or wax is used to resist the dye, and are sometimes used in tie-dyeing. (The fiber-reactive dyes listed below are not suitable for tie-dyeing except when the folding-and-dipping method is used.)

Most dyes adhere to the fiber better if they are as warm as possible when applied. Wax resists will withstand heat up to at least 115°F., and some have an even higher melting point. A cold dyebath should be about 100°F. when the fabric is entered. Since the cold dyebath is concentrated and the dyeing time is short, it is especially important to move the fabric continuously in the bath to avoid spots and streaks.

Because fabric dyed in a cold bath is not fixed until it has been steamed, it should not be rinsed after dyeing, and it should be dried before fixation procedures are begun (unless otherwise specified in the directions). If the piece is hung on a line to dry, excess color collects and darkens the lower areas of the fabric. It is safer to shake away as much excess liquid as possible upon removal from the bath and then to lay the fabric on a plastic-covered table to dry.

BASIC DYES

Cotton, linen, and viscose rayon

These fabrics must be premordanted by either of the methods described on page 140.
      X% dyestuff
      ½% glacial acetic acid
      10 to 1 liquor ratio
Method:

The dyestuff is pasted with the acetic acid, and enough hot water to dissolve it is added. A third of this solution is stirred into the bath at 20-minute intervals; the fabric is removed and re-entered for each addition. The dyeing is continued for 20 minutes after the last addition.

Silk and wool
Method:

The same as for cotton, linen, and viscose rayon, without premordanting.

FIBER-REACTIVE DYES

The formula given here is for the especially sensitive group of fiber-reactive dyes known as the Procion M series (manufactured by I.C.I./Organics/ Inc.).

A special treatment is required for fabric to be decorated with these dyes. The fabric is entered in a bath of 3 teaspoons Synthrapol SP per 2 gallons of water, and the temperature is raised to about 170°F. (105°F. maximum for silk and wool). The fabric is moved about in the bath for 30 minutes. It is then removed, rinsed thoroughly, and dried.

Cotton, linen, viscose rayon, silk, and wool
      X% dyestuff
    20 to 55% common salt
      9% washing soda
    20 to 1 liquor ratio

The following table may be used to determine the amount of dyestuff and salt for the shade desired:

Color Value	% of Dyestuff	% of Salt
Deep	7%	55%
Medium	4%	40%
Pale	1%	20%

Method:

The dyestuff is pasted with a small amount of cold water, and enough hot water (not over 140°F.) to dissolve it is added. This solution is stirred into the bath. The fabric is entered and moved about continuously for 10 to 15 minutes. A third of the salt is stirred into the bath at 5-minute intervals; the fabric is removed and re-entered for each addition. The fabric is moved about in the bath for 20 minutes after the last addition. The washing soda, dissolved in a small amount of warm water, is now stirred into the bath. The fabric is re-entered and kept moving about for 10 minutes. The dyeing is then continued for 1 hour. The fabric is removed from the bath, as much of the excess liquid as possible is shaken out, and the fabric is spread smoothly over a plastic-covered table to dry.

These fiber-reactive dyes can be fixed with a minimum of steaming in any type of steamer. However, they can also be satisfactorily fixed by any of the following simple methods: (1) hanging the fabric in a warm, damp atmosphere for several hours (a bathroom in which a hot shower is turned on from time to time is an ideal place); (2) ironing the fabric for 5 minutes with a regular or steam iron; (3) tumbling the fabric in a laundry dryer set at high temperature for 30 to 45 minutes.

The fabric must be finished by entering it in a bath of 3 teaspoons Synthrapol SP per 2 gallons of water. The temperature is raised to about 170°F., and the fabric is moved about for 5 minutes. It is then rinsed thoroughly and dried.

BRENTAMINE FAST BLACK K SALT

This product of I.C.I./Organics/Inc. can be used by itself to create brown hues, or to overdye the Procion M series for color variation.

Cotton, linen, viscose rayon, silk, and wool

The fabric must be pretreated as described above for the fiber-reactive Procion M series dyes.

> .2 teaspoons Brentamine Fast Black K salt per quart of water
>> 1 teaspoon common salt
> 5 to 1 liquor ratio

Method:

The dyestuff is pasted in a small amount of cold water. This mixture is added to the bath, which should never be over 85°F. The fabric is entered and moved about in the bath until the desired depth of color is achieved. The fabric is removed and spread smoothly over a plastic-covered table to dry. It must be fixed and finished as described above for the fiber-reactive Procion M series dyes.

SOLUBLE VAT DYES

Cotton, linen, and viscose rayon

> X% dyestuff
> 2% Glauber's salt
>> 1 gram sodium nitrate per quart of water
>> 4 teaspoons sulfuric acid per quart of water
> 5 to 1 liquor ratio

Method:

The dyestuff is dissolved in a small amount of lukewarm water and added to the bath. The fabric is entered and moved about for 20 minutes. Half the salt is stirred in at 20-minute intervals; the fabric is removed and re-entered for each addition. Then it is immediately entered in the bath of sodium nitrate, left for 1 minute, and immediately entered in the developing bath of sulfuric acid. The fabric is moved about until the color has developed. It is rinsed in cold water, washed in a hot detergent bath, and rinsed again.

MINERAL COLORS

Cotton and linen

Permanganate of potash (light to dark yellow-ochre)

>> 1 teaspoon permanganate of potash per quart of water
> 5 to 1 liquor ratio

Method:

The permanganate of potash is dissolved in a small amount of hot water, and the solution is added to the bath. The fabric is entered and moved about until the desired color value is achieved. It is rinsed in cold water.

Ferrous sulfate and lead acetate (red-brown)

>> 454 grams ferrous sulfate per 5 quarts of hot water
>> 227 grams lead acetate
>> 125 grams caustic soda per 5 quarts of cold water
> 5 to 1 liquor ratio

Method:

The ferrous sulfate is dissolved in the hot water,

and the lead acetate is stirred in. The mixture is left for 6 or 8 hours. The green liquid that will have formed over a white sediment is carefully poured into another container so that the sediment is not disturbed. (The sediment is thoroughly washed out of the container immediately.) The fabric is entered in the bath and moved about from time to time. After 1 hour, the fabric is removed, wrung out, and laid on a plastic-covered table to dry. When dry, it is entered in the developing bath of caustic soda. The fabric is moved about for 2 minutes, removed, wrung out, and laid on the plastic-covered table again. When the color is evenly developed, the fabric is rinsed in cold water, washed in a hot detergent bath, and rinsed again.

Dye Pastes

Dyestuffs must be made into pastes in order to be applied to definite design areas of the fabric. Pastes are required for printing and painting and other direct techniques of fabric decoration.

The formulas for the pastes contain dyestuff, assistants, and an amount of thickener which may be varied to achieve the consistency needed for a particular use.

Thickeners are made of various gums or starches combined with water. The formulas for thickeners given here are intended as guides. The craftsman must experiment to find the consistency most useful for the project at hand. The paste should be as thin as possible without actually running beyond the edges of the design areas. A paste which is too thick may deposit excess dye that will migrate outside the design area during fixation. It is more difficult to fix and to wash out during finishing. A very thick paste will also dry too rapidly in the screen and clog the mesh. In general, however, a thin fabric needs a slightly more viscous paste, while a thick fabric needs a thinner one if it is to penetrate the fibers.

The following table shows the thickeners used with the various classes of dyestuffs:

Gum arabic thickener
> 600 parts gum arabic lumps
> 1,000 parts cold water

Method:

The gum arabic is stirred into the water and left to soak for 2 or 3 days. It should be stirred occasionally, and any foreign particles which rise to the top should be skimmed off. The mixture is then placed in a double boiler and heated for 3 or 4 hours, with frequent stirring. It is left to stand for another 2 or 3 days. It is then strained into a new container carefully, so that any sediment is not disturbed. More water may be added to thin.

Gum tragacanth thickener
> 70 parts gum tragacanth
> 1,000 parts cold water

Method:

The gum tragacanth is sprinkled on the surface of the water and left for 2 or 3 days. It should be stirred occasionally. The mixture is then placed in a double boiler and heated for 8 hours, with occasional stirring. Water is added to the mixture and to the bottom of the double boiler from time to time to replace loss by evaporation. More water may be added to thin.

Sodium alginate thickener
> 10 parts Calgon
> 50 parts sodium alginate grains
> 1,000 parts cold water

Method:

The Calgon is dissolved in a small amount of warm water. The cold water is added, and the sodium alginate is sprinkled in while the mixture is stirred briskly so that lumps do not form. The mixture is stirred for 5 or 10 minutes more and then left for 1 hour, or until it appears smooth and glassy. More water may be added to thin.

Thickener	Acid dyes	Basic dyes	Direct dyes	Disperse dyes	Fiber-reactive dyes	Soluble vat dyes	Household dyes
Gum Arabic	X	X					
Gum Tragacanth	X	X	X				X
Sodium Alginate	X				X	X	
Sodium Alginate-Emulsion				X	X		
Starch-Tragacanth		X					

Sodium alginate-emulsion thickener
      16 parts Lubrol PR-G
      540 parts water
      460 parts mineral spirits
Method:

The Lubrol PR-G is dissolved in the water by mixing with a mechanical beater. The mineral spirits are added very gradually, mixing at high speed. If any separation of the oil occurs, a thorough beating will restore the mixture to its original state. This emulsion is mixed with the sodium alginate thickening when the dye paste is made up.

Starch-tragacanth thickener
      100 parts laundry starch
      1,000 parts cold water
      50 parts olive oil
Method:

A smooth paste is made with the starch and a small amount of the water. The remainder of the water and the oil are added and stirred briskly. The mixture is placed in a double boiler and heated and stirred until thick. It is removed from the heat and stirred until cool. It is then mixed with the gum tragacanth thickener in a ratio of 1 part starch mixture to 2 parts gum tragacanth thickener. A mixture of 1 to 1 will give a less sticky consistency. More water may be added to thin.

It should be noted that the number of parts of dyestuff in the following formulas for dye pastes varies (indicating light to dark color values), and water should be added after the paste has been mixed to make up a full 1,000 parts. A 1,000-gram formula is suggested for a one-color print covering approximately two-thirds of the surface of a 3-yard length of fabric.

ACID DYES
   Silk, wool, and nylon
      10 to 40 parts dyestuff
         50 parts glycerin (reduce by half for silk)
         300 parts water
         600 parts thickener (gum tragacanth or gum arabic)
         25 parts tartaric acid
         25 parts water
Method:

The dyestuff is mixed with the glycerin, and the water is added. The mixture is heated until the dyestuff is dissolved. This solution is cooled and stirred into the thickener. The tartaric acid, dissolved in the water, is added. After the paste has been applied,

the fabric is dried and then steamed for 1 hour. It is rinsed thoroughly in cold water, washed carefully in lukewarm water to which a small amount of Synthrapol SP has been added, and rinsed again in cold water.

BASIC DYES
   Cotton, linen, and viscose rayon
      10 to 40 parts dyestuff
         50 parts Glydote B
         40 parts glacial acetic acid
         170 parts hot water
         20 parts tartaric acid
         600 parts thickener (gum arabic, gum tragacanth, or starch-tragacanth)
         50 parts tannic-acetic acid (equal parts of tannic acid and glacial acetic acid diluted with water in a 1-to-3 ratio)
Method:

The dyestuff is mixed with the Glydote B and acetic acid. The hot water is added, and the tartaric acid is stirred in. This solution is stirred in the thickener and left to cool. The tannic-acetic acid is stirred in. After the paste has been applied, the fabric is dried and then steamed for 1 hour. It is then immersed for 30 seconds in a deep bath of 10 parts tartar emetic per 1,000 parts water at 120°F., and rinsed in cold water.

   Silk and wool
      10 to 20 parts dyestuff
         25 parts glycerin
         25 parts glacial acetic acid
         25 parts cold water
         340 parts hot water
         525 parts thickener (gum arabic or gum tragacanth)
         25 parts tartaric acid
         50 parts water
Method:

A paste is made of the dyestuff, glycerin, acetic acid, and cold water. The hot water is added, and this solution is stirred into the thickener. The tartaric acid, dissolved in the water, is added. After the paste has been applied, the fabric is dried, steamed for 1 hour, and rinsed in lukewarm water.

DIRECT DYES
   Cotton, linen, viscose rayon, silk, and wool
      10 to 20 parts dyestuff
         50 parts urea
         350 parts hot water

565 parts thickener (gum tragacanth or sodium alginate)

15 parts disodium hydrogen phosphate

Method:

The dyestuff is mixed with the urea, and the hot water is added. This solution is stirred into the thickener, and the disodium hydrogen phosphate is added. After the paste has been applied, the fabric is dried, steamed for 1 hour, and rinsed in lukewarm water.

FIBER-REACTIVE DYES (Procion M series)

Cotton, linen, viscose rayon, and silk

5 to 70 parts dyestuff

50 to 150 parts urea

190 to 270 parts hot water

650 parts sodium alginate thickener

12.5 parts sodium bicarbonate (except for Procion Brilliant Blue H 5GS, which requires 30 parts)

The following table may be used to determine the amount of dyestuff and urea for the shade desired:

Color Value	Dyestuff	Urea
Deep	40 to 70 parts	150 parts
Medium	10 to 40 parts	100 parts
Pale	5 to 10 parts	50 parts

Method:

A stock paste without color is mixed by dissolving the urea in the hot water. This solution is stirred into the combined thickeners. (This paste is usable for several weeks if it is stored in a tightly closed glass jar; it may be kept indefinitely if it is refrigerated.) When the paste is to be applied, the dyestuff is added and is left to dissolve for 5 minutes. Immediately prior to application, the sodium bicarbonate is stirred in. After the paste has been applied, the fabric is dried and then steamed for 5 to 15 minutes. It is finished by rinsing first in cold, then in hot water, and boiling for 5 minutes in a bath to which a small amount of Synthrapol SP has been added. If the water becomes excessively colored, the fabric should be removed and placed in a fresh bath.

RESIST PASTES WITH FIBER-REACTIVE DYES

A variety of unusual color effects can be obtained on cotton fabrics by printing a resist paste in the design areas and then overprinting with Procion M fiber-reactive dye pastes. The specific colors to be used with resist pastes will be recommended by the manufacturer.

White resist

10 parts Nacan

50 to 100 parts titanium dioxide (ground into a paste with an equal amount of water, using a mortar and pestle)

100 parts Fixapret CP

400 parts sodium alginate thickener

10 parts ammonium dihydrogen phosphate

350 to 400 parts water (160°F.)

Method:

The Nacan is dissolved in an equal amount of hot water and then stirred into the titanium dioxide paste. The Fixapret CP is added, and this mixture is stirred into the thickener. The ammonium dihydrogen phosphate, dissolved in the water, is stirred into the thickening mixture. The paste is applied to the fabric, which should be dried as quickly as possible (preferably with a fan) and placed in a laundry dryer set at high temperature for 1 hour. The fabric is then overprinted with a fiber-reactive dye paste, dried, and steamed for 30 to 45 minutes. It is finished by rinsing first in cold, then hot water, boiling 5 minutes in a bath to which a small amount of Synthrapol SP has been added, and rinsing again. It will be seen that the design areas have resisted the color printed over them.

Color resist

30 to 60 parts dyestuff

420 parts water (maximum temperature 160°F.)

400 parts sodium alginate thickener

10 parts Nacan

100 parts Fixapret CP

20 parts Procion Resin Catalyst A

Method:

The dyestuff is dissolved in the hot water, and the solution is stirred into the thickener. The Nacan is dissolved in an equal amount of hot water and mixed with the Fixapret CP and the Procion Resin Catalyst A. This mixture is stirred into the dye paste. (It should be noted that urea and sodium bicarbonate must never be mixed with the dye used in resist pastes.) The paste is applied to the fabric, which should be dried as quickly as possible (preferably with a fan) and placed in a laundry dryer set at high temperature for 1 hour. The fabric is then overprinted with a fiber-reactive dye paste, dried, and steamed for 30 to 45 minutes. It is finished by rinsing first in cold, then hot water, boiling 5 minutes in a bath to which a small amount of Synthrapol SP has been added, and rinsing again.

HOUSEHOLD DYES

Cotton, linen, and viscose rayon

    10 to 20 parts dyestuff
        10 parts Glauber's salt
       100 parts glycerin
       300 parts water
       500 parts gum tragacanth thickener

Method:

The dyestuff is mixed with the Glauber's salt and glycerin, the water is added, and the mixture is heated until the dyestuff is dissolved. The solution is cooled and stirred into the thickener. After the paste has been applied, the fabric is dried, steamed for 30 to 45 minutes, and rinsed in lukewarm water.

Silk and wool

    10 to 20 parts dyestuff
       100 parts glycerin
       100 parts vinegar
       200 parts water
       500 parts gum tragacanth thickener

Method:

The dyestuff is mixed with the glycerin and vinegar, the water is added, and the mixture is heated until the dyestuff is dissolved. The solution is cooled and stirred into the thickener. After the paste has been applied, the fabric is dried, steamed for 30 to 45 minutes, and rinsed in lukewarm water.

PREPARED VAT DYES

The vat dyes sold under the brand name Inko are already thickened to a consistency suitable for printing or painting.

Cotton, linen, viscose rayon, and silk
Method:

A clear extender is available for lightening the color values. After the paste has been applied, the fabric is either dried and fixed by steaming for 1 hour, or fixed by ironing with a hand iron. If the latter method is used, newsprint or paper towels should be spread over the slightly damp (but not wet) printed areas and ironed until the color has oxidized and the print is dry.

SOLUBLE VAT DYES

Cotton, linen, and viscose rayon

    10 to 50 parts dyestuff
        50 parts urea
        50 parts water
       800 parts sodium alginate thickener
        50 parts sodium nitrate solution, 30% (30
             parts sodium nitrate to 70 parts water)

Method:

The dyestuff and urea are mixed together, the water is added, and the mixture is heated to 175°F. This solution is stirred into the thickener, and the sodium nitrate solution is added. After the paste has been applied, the fabric is dried and steamed for 15 minutes. The fabric is immersed completely in a bath of 36 parts sulfuric acid per 1,000 parts water at 160°F., and it is moved about for a few seconds. The fabric is removed and exposed to the air for 30 seconds. It is finished by rinsing in several baths of cold water, boiling for 15 minutes in a detergent bath, and rinsing again.

Discharge Methods

When a light design on a dark ground is required, a method of discharging some of the ground color is used. Cotton, linen, and viscose rayon dyed with direct dyes, as well as some commercially dyed fabrics, are suitable for color discharging in baths of household bleach. This method is especially suitable for tie-dye and wax-resist techniques.

Pastes containing a bleaching substance can be used with printing and painting techniques. They are applied on fabrics dyed with direct, fiber-reactive, vat, or mineral color dyes before the dyed fabric has been fixed and finished. The dye manufacturer will recommend the specific colors suitable for use with discharge methods.

DISCHARGE BATH

Cotton, linen, and viscose rayon

       250 parts liquid household bleach
       750 parts cold water
         5 to 1 liquor ratio

Method:

The wet-out fabric is entered in the bath and moved about continuously until the desired lightness of value is achieved. It is removed, rinsed in cold water, washed in a hot detergent bath, and rinsed again. (If more bleach is used, the time required will be shorter, but the fiber may be harmed.)

DISCHARGE PASTE OVER DIRECT DYES

Cotton, linen, and viscose rayon

       150 parts sodium sulphoxylate formaldehyde
        50 parts glycerin
       200 parts cold water
       600 parts gum tragacanth thickener

Method:

The sodium sulphoxylate formaldehyde is mixed with the glycerin, and the water is added. This solution is stirred into the thickener. After the paste has been applied, the fabric is dried, steamed for 5 minutes, and rinsed thoroughly in several baths of lukewarm water.

<small>DISCHARGE PASTE OVER FIBER-REACTIVE DYES</small>

Cotton, linen, and viscose rayon

    150 parts sodium sulphoxylate formaldehyde
    50 parts Metabol WS
    50 parts Solution Salt BN 200
    25 parts soda ash
    100 parts zinc oxide (ground into a paste with 100 parts of thickener, using a mortar and pestle)
    525 parts gum tragacanth thickener

Method:

The sodium sulphoxylate formaldehyde, Metabol WS, Solution Salt, and soda ash are mixed together and stirred into the zinc oxide paste. This mixture is added to the thickener. After the paste has been applied, the fabric is dried and steamed for 5 to 10 minutes. It is then rinsed in cold water, boiled in a bath to which a small amount of Synthrapol SP has been added, and rinsed again.

<small>DISCHARGE PASTE OVER PERMANGANATE OF POTASH</small>

Cotton, linen, and viscose rayon

    250 parts lemon juice
    750 parts gum tragacanth thickener

Method:

The juice is stirred into the thickener and applied to the fabric. It is dried, rinsed in cold water, boiled in a detergent bath, and rinsed again. (Varying the proportion of lemon juice to thickener will vary the lightness of value achieved.)

<small>PREPARED DISCHARGE PASTE OVER VAT DYES</small>

Cotton, linen, and viscose rayon

A ready-to-use discharge paste is available under the Inko brand name. After the paste is applied, the fabric is dried and steamed for 10 to 15 minutes. It is rinsed in cold water, boiled in a detergent bath, and rinsed again.

Color Stripping

It is often necessary to remove a color from a fabric which has been unsatisfactorily dyed. Color removers packaged by household dye manufacturers may be used successfully.

Sodium hydrosulfite, available from laundry or chemical supply houses, may also be kept in the studio for color stripping.

Method:

The fabric is entered in a water bath, and the temperature is raised to 190°F. The fabric is removed, and 3 tablespoons of sodium hydrosulfite per 4 gallons of water are stirred into the bath. The fabric is re-entered and moved about for 15 to 20 minutes or until free of color. If cotton or rayon fabrics retain some color, they may be further treated by immersing them in a weak solution of household bleach. When the fabric is removed from the bleach, it is rinsed and washed thoroughly in a detergent bath.

Pigment Pastes

The craftsman may choose from a number of brands of textile pigments in each of the following classifications: emulsion pigments, synthetic-base pigments, and oil-based pigments. Each brand will be supplied with specific directions and ready-to-use compounds that are combined with the pigment. Among these compounds are extender, transparent base, thinner or reducer, and retarder. An extender is used to add bulk and hardness to the pigment. With some brands the extender is used to produce transparent color, while with others a special transparent base is provided for this purpose. The manufacturer will recommend certain ratios of extender or transparent base to pigment for specific color effects.

Consistency and drying time are factors to be considered in work with pigments. The proper consistency for the technique being used can be achieved by addition of extender and the recommended thinner. If thinner is added, however, the drying time will be shortened, and the pigment may dry in the screen, clogging the mesh. Retarders are usually available to slow the drying time, and experimentation will result in the proper paste mixture.

The emulsion pigments are of special interest for several reasons. Some brands call for water as a thinner and as a solvent for clean-up. This is a great convenience, and it is also less expensive than purchasing solvents such as mineral spirits. The same brands give directions for extenders that the craftsman can mix himself, which is less expensive than purchasing them.

Oil-based printer's inks and block printing inks can be used on fabrics; however, if they are not sold specifically for this purpose, non-fugitive (non-fading) brands should be specified. Two types of white are available in these inks: an opaque cover white and a transparent mixing base. The opaque white is used to produce tints and dense pigments that will cover the ground color of the fabric. The mixing base is used to produce transparent effects similar to those achieved with extender. These pigments are best mixed on a glass or metal palette with a long-bladed metal spatula. If the ink is too thick for proper coating of the brayer, a drop or two of linseed oil may be added. Too much oil, however, will cause the pigment to bleed when printed, resulting in fuzzy edges.

Chemicals and Assistants

A variety of assistants and other chemicals are called for in the formulas given for dyebaths, dye pastes, and thickenings. A number of chemicals are also required for pretreatments and aftertreatments of fabrics. Most are available at local pharmacies or drug supply houses. A few are sold under brand names; these are indicated with an asterisk.

Acetic acid is an exhausting agent used with several dyestuffs. The concentrated, or glacial, type is usually required. Vinegar is a weak form of acetic acid.

Alcohol is used to help dissolve basic dyes.

Ammonium acetate neutralizes residual alkalinity which may cause a fiber to resist acid dyes.

Ammonium dihydrogen phosphate is used in resist pastes with fiber-reactive dyes to help resist subsequent dyeing.

Brentamine Fast Black K Salt* is a coloring agent used with fiber-reactive dyes.

Calgon* (sodium hexametaphosphate) is a water softener.

Caustic soda is used to develop the color when dyeing with ferrous sulfate.

Common salt (sodium chloride) creates an affinity between several dyestuffs and fibers. It acts as a retardant with some dyestuffs.

Disodium hydrogen phosphate is a mordant used with direct dyes.

Fixapret CP* is used in resist pastes with fiber-reactive dyes.

Glauber's salt creates an affinity between several dyestuffs and fibers. It acts as a retardant with some dyestuffs.

Glycerin is used to help dissolve several dyestuffs.

Glydote B* is used to help dissolve basic dyes.

Lead acetate is used to aid in coloring fabric with ferrous sulfate.

Metabol WS* is used in discharge pastes with fiber-reactive dyes.

Nacan* is used to prevent decomposition of fiber-reactive dyes during fixation.

Procion Resin Catalyst A* is used in resist pastes with fiber-reactive dyes when a color is included in the paste.

Salsoda* (washing soda) increases the solubility of fiber-reactive dyes in water.

Sitol Flakes* is a chemical used to prevent decomposition of fiber-reactive dyes during fixation.

Soda ash is used in discharge pastes with fiber-reactive dyes.

Sodium bicarbonate is required for the fixation of fiber-reactive dyes.

Sodium hydrosulfite is a bleaching agent. Household color removers are composed of this chemical.

Sodium nitrate is used as an oxidizing agent with vat dyes.

Sodium sulphoxylate formaldehyde is used in discharge pastes.

Solution Salt BN 200* is used in discharge pastes with fiber-reactive dyes.

Sulfuric acid is used to develop the color with vat dyes and to exhaust color with acid dyes.

Synthetic detergents (household liquid detergents) are required for the use of several dyestuffs.

Synthrapol SP* is a synthetic detergent and a fabric softener. Pretreatment of fabric with this chemical increases the affinity between the dyestuff and the fiber.

Tannic acid is a mordant used with several dyestuffs.

Tartaric acid is used in dye pastes with acid dyes.

Tartar emetic is used with tannic acid as a mordant with basic dyes.

Titanium dioxide is used in resist pastes with fiber-reactive dyes to secure a good white.

Urea is used to help dissolve and fix several dyestuffs.

Zinc oxide is used in discharge pastes with fiber-reactive dyes to secure a good white.

Glossary

Aftertreatment—Any process a fabric may require after the application of dye, such as fixation and finishing.

Assistant—Chemical that aids in creating the bond between dye and fiber.

Back-tanning—Mordanting a dyed fabric which has been premordanted with tannic acid.

Batik—Technique of decoration in which hot wax is applied to the fabric to resist subsequent coloring.

Binder—Substance in which pigments are suspended to make a paste.

Bleeding—Running of color from a dyed fabric when dampened.

Blockout—Substance used to fill the mesh of a screen to prevent passage of the printing medium in screen printing.

Block Printing—Technique of decoration in which the fabric is printed by hand with wood or linoleum blocks.

Butt Joint—Method of printing repeats so that they meet along a straight line.

Cellulosic Fiber—Fiber obtained from a plant, such as cotton or linen.

Cold Dyeing—Process of coloring fabric in a bath at about 100°F.

Color Separation—Procedure by which the various colors of a design are isolated for printing one at a time.

Crackle—Fine-line effects produced in the wax-resist technique.

Discharge—Removal of some or all of the color from a fabric.

Discharge Paste—Paste containing a bleaching substance for removing color from a fabric.

Dovetail Joint—Method of printing repeats so that a portion of one unit fits into a part of the next without touching it.

Dyebath—Solution of dyestuff, assistants, and water in which fabrics are colored.

Dye Paste—Viscous mixture of dyestuff, chemicals, and thickener used to color fabrics in printing and painting techniques.

Dyestuff—Material that colors fabrics by combining chemically with the fiber.

Dye Uptake—Absorption of the colorant by the fiber.

Exhaust—To cause total absorption of color from a dyebath by the fiber.

Exhausting Agent—Chemical which promotes the absorption of color from the dyebath by the fiber.

Extender—Paste used to reduce the color value of a dye or pigment paste.

Fastness—Ability of a dye or pigment to withstand washing, boiling, or exposure to light.

Finishing—Process of washing, rinsing, and ironing decorated fabrics.

Fixation—Process by which colors are permanently fixed in or attached to the fiber of a decorated fabric.

Flock—Finely shredded fiber used to give an absorbent surface to wood and lineloum blocks.

Ground Color—Original color of a decorated fabric.

Hot Dyeing—Process of coloring fabric in a heated bath.

Immersion Dyeing—Process of coloring a fabric in which the fabric is submerged in the bath.

Level Dyeing—Even coloring of a fabric.

Liquor Ratio—Amount of water in a dyebath in relation to the weight of the fabric to be dyed.

Mercerizing Process—Finishing process used for cotton goods to increase their luster and strengthen and improve their affinity with dyes.

Migration—Spreading of color outside the area of application.

Mordant—Substance which creates an affinity between dye and fiber.

Overdyeing—Dyeing over previously dyed areas with another color.

Overlapping Joint—Method of printing repeats in which a portion of one unit overlaps a portion of the next unit.

Overprinting—Printing over previously printed areas with the same or another color.

Pattern Book—Collection of samples of dyed fabric with formulas and technical information.

Permanent Blockout—Stencil material, not affected by the printing medium, used to fill the mesh of a screen to prevent passage of the medium in screen printing.

Pigment—Material that colors fabric by coating the fiber.

Pretreatment—Any process by which fabric is prepared for the application of dye.

Reducer—See *Thinner.*

Registration—Exact alignment of one repeat with another in printing.

Registration Mark—Visible indicator used as a guide in printing.

Remover—Liquid used to clean a stencil material from a screen in screen printing.

Repeat—Basic unit of design in fabric decoration.

Resist—Process or material which prevents dye from reaching designated areas of a fabric.

Retardant—Chemical that delays the absorption of dye by a fiber.

Screen Printing—Technique of decoration in which color is forced onto the fabric through a stencil attached to a screen made of fabric stretched on a frame.

Size—Substance applied to fabric to give it added strength or body.

Solvent—Liquid used to remove stencil materials in screen printing and dissolve media for clean-up.

Squeegee—Tool with a wooden handle and a rubber blade used to force the printing medium through the mesh of a screen in screen printing.

Stamping—Means of transferring a design to fabric by pressing a color-coated object onto its surface.

Stencil—Thin material perforated with a design through which a printing medium is forced onto the fabric to be decorated.

Stiffness of Hand—Inflexibility of fabric to the touch.

Straight of the Weave—Following the warp or weft threads of a fabric.

Stripping—Removal of color from a dyed fabric by chemical means.

Synthetic Fiber—Fiber produced by chemical synthesis.

Temporary Blockout—Stencil material used to fill the mesh of a screen in areas subsequently to be opened to permit passage of the printing medium in screen printing.

Thickener—Substance made with a gum or starch and added to dye pastes to achieve the consistency needed for application to a fabric.

Thinner—Liquid used to thin the consistency of a dye or pigment paste.

Tie-dye—Technique of decoration in which the fabric is bound so it will resist color in designated areas.

Warp—Longitudinal yarns in woven fabric.

Weft—Crosswise yarns in woven fabric.

Wet-out—To thoroughly dampen fabric before dyeing.

Suppliers

Riko's Art Materials
714 North Wabash Ave.
Chicago, Ill. 60611

Advance Process Supply Co.
400 North Noble Street
Chicago, Ill. 60622

BAST Wyandotte, Corp.
100 Cherry Hill Road
Parsippany, N.J. 07054

Craftools, Inc.
1 Industrial Road
Woodbridge, N.J. 07075

Colonial Printing Ink Co.
182 E. Union Avenue
East Rutherford, N.J. 07073

Dadant & Sons, Inc.
Hamilton, Illinois 62341

Dharma Trading Co.
P.O. Box 916 C
San Rafael, Ca. 94902

Fab/Dec
3553 Old Post Road
San Angelo, Texas 76901

Farquhar Fabric Dyes
6 Clarence Square
Toronto 135, Ont., Canada

Hilton-Davis Chemical Co.
P.O. Box 1117
Greenville, South Carolina

ICI United States, Inc.
Concord Pike & New Murphy Rd.
Wilmington, Del. 19899

Keystone Aniline & Chemical Co.
321 N. Loomis Street
Chicago, Ill. 60607

The Naz-Dar Company
1087 N. North Branch St.
Chicago, Ill. 60622

Northwest Handcraft House Ltd.
110 W. Esplanada
North Vancouver, B.C., Canada

Pylam Products Co.
95-10 218th St.
Queens Village, N.Y. 11429

Resin Coatings Corp.
14840 N.W. 25th Court
Opa Locka, Fla. 33054

Rupert, Gibbon and Spider
470 Maylin
Pasadena, Calif. 91105

Celanese Coatings & Specialty Co.
2877 Five Springs Rd.
Dalton, Georgia 30720

Screen Process Supplies
1199 East 12th Street
Oakland, Calif. 94606

Wax, tjantings, rice and
starch paste ingredients

All screen printing supplies,
pigments

Fixapret CP and other chemicals,
also pigments

Wax, tjantings, stretchers

Beeswax in large amounts

Procion fiber reactive dyes,
fabrics, tjantings, wax,
thickener

Procion fiber reactive dyes,
sodium alginate thickener, fabrics,
urea

Dylan fiber reactive dyes

Seabond colors

Glydote B, Fixapret, Resin
Catalyst A, Metabol WS, Solution
Salt BN, Procion fiber reactive dyes

Variety of dyes

All screen printing supplies,
pigments

Fabrics, fiber reactive dyes,

Fiber reactive dyes

Remy's Resist

Deka Colors, pigments

Halltex Sodium Aiginate
thickener in large amounts

Ready-to-use vat dyes,
all screen printing supplies

Bibliography

Albeck, Pat. *Printed Textiles*, London, Oxford University Press, 1969.

American Fabrics Magazine, Editors of. *Encyclopedia of Textiles*. Englewood Cliffs, New Jersey: Prentice-Hall Inc., 1960.

Anderson, Donald M. *Elements of Design.* New York: Holt, Rinehart & Winston, 1961.

Ballinger, Louise B., and Vroman, Thomas F. *Design: Sources and Resources.* New York: Reinhold Publishing Corp., 1965.

Beitler, Ethel Jane, and Lockhart, Bill. *Design For You.* New York: John Wiley and Sons, Inc., 1961.

Born, W. "Textile Ornament," *Ciba Review* #37. The Society of Chemical Industry in Basle, January, 1941.

Bhushan, Jamila B. *The Costumes and·Textiles of India.* Bombay: D. B. Taraporevala & Sons, 1958.

Bird, Junius. *Paracas Fabrics & Nazca Needlework.* Washington, D. C.: National Publishing Co., 1954.

Birren, Faber. *Creative Color.* New York: Reinhold Publishing Corp., 1961.

Brief Guide to Oriental Painted, Dyed and Printed Textiles. London: Victoria and Albert Museum, H. M. Stationary Office, 1950.

Briggs, Asa (ed.). *William Morris Selected Writings and Designs.* Baltimore: Pelican Books, 1962.

Collier, Graham. *Form, Space and Vision.* Englewood Cliffs, New Jersey: Prentice-Hall Inc., 1963.

Conran, Terence. *Printed Textile Design.* London: The Studio Publications, 1957.

The Cooper Union Museum Chronicle, Vol. 3, No. 5 (October, 1963).

Design by the Yard, Textile Printing from 800–1956. New York: The Cooper Union Museum, 1956.

D'Harcourt, Raoul. *Textiles of Ancient Peru and Their Techniques.* Seattle: University of Washington Press, 1962.

Emerson, Sybil. *Design: A Creative Approach.* Scranton: International Text Book Co., 1955.

Erickson, Janet. *Block Printing on Textiles.* New York: Watson-Guptill Publications, 1961.

Hunter, George L. *Decorative Textiles.* Philadelphia: J. B. Lippincott Co., 1918.

Imperial Chemical Industries Ltd. *An Introduction to Textile Printing.* Washington, D. C.: Butterworth Inc., 1964.

————. *Procion Dyestuffs in Textile Dyeing.* Great Britain: Imperial Chemical Industries Dyestuffs Division, 1962.

Jacobson, Egbert. *Basic Color.* Chicago: Paul Theobald, 1948.

Joseph, Marjory L. *Introductory Textile Science.* New York: Holt, Rinehart & Winston, 1966.

Kosloff, Albert. *Screen Process Printing.* Cincinnati: The Signs of the Times Publishing Co., 1958.

Krevitski, Nik. *Batik: Art and Craft.* New York: Reinhold Publishing Corp., 1964.

Kümpers, Hilde. *Kunst auf Baumwolle.* Dortmund: Ardey-Velag, 1961.

Langewis, Laurens, and Wagner, Fritz A. *Decorative Art in Indonesian Textiles.* Amsterdam: Uitgeverij C. P. J. Van der Peet, 1964.

Maile, Anne. *Tie and Dye.* London: Mills & Boon Ltd., 1963.

Means, Philip Ainsworth. *A Study of Peruvian Textiles.* Boston: The Museum of Fine Arts, 1932.

Nelson, George. *Problems of Design.* New York: Whitney Publications, 1957.

Nihon Sen'i Isho Senta. *Textile Designs of Japan,* Vol. I (1959) and Vol. III (1961). Osaka: Japan Textile Color Design Center.

Osumi, Tamezo. *Printed Cottons of Asia.* Tokyo and Rutland, Vermont: Bijutsu Shuppan-Shu and Charles E. Tuttle, 1963.

Percival, MacIver. *The Chintz Book.* New York: Stokes Co., n.d.

Proctor, Richard M. *The Principles of Pattern,* New York, Van Nostrand Reinhold Company, 1969.

Proud, Nora. *Textile Printing and Dyeing.* New York: Reinhold Publishing Corp., 1965.

Röttger, Ernst. *Creative Paper Design.* New York: Reinhold Publishing Corp., 1961.

Russ, Stephen. *Fabric Printing by Hand.* New York: Watson-Guptill Publications, 1965.

Trowell, Margaret. *African Designs.* (2nd ed.). New York: Frederick A. Praeger, 1966.

Index